CATS OF AFRICA

CATS
OF AFRICA

TEXT BY ANTHONY HALL-MARTIN

PAINTINGS AND DRAWINGS BY PAUL BOSMAN

SMITHSONIAN INSTITUTION PRESS

WASHINGTON, D.C.

NOTE ON THE TAXONOMY OF AFRICAN CATS

The taxonomy of the cat family, the Felidae, is still not entirely settled.
In this book we have followed the work of Wozencroft (1993),
but regard the African wild cat as a full subspecies of *Felis silvestris*.

TEXT © 1997 ANTHONY HALL-MARTIN
PAINTINGS AND DRAWINGS © 1997 PAUL BOSMAN
ALL RIGHTS RESERVED

FIRST PUBLISHED IN THE UNITED STATES OF AMERICA
BY SMITHSONIAN INSTITUTION PRESS IN 1998
ISBN 1-56098-760-X

LIBRARY OF CONGRESS CATALOG NUMBER IS AVAILABLE

PUBLISHED IN SOUTH AFRICA BY FERNWOOD PRESS (PTY) LTD, CAPE TOWN
DESIGNED BY WILLEM JORDAAN
EDITED BY PETER BORCHERT AND LAURA MILTON
MAPWORK BY PETER BOSMAN
INDEX BY LEONIE TWENTYMAN JONES
PRODUCTION CONTROL BY ABDUL LATIEF (BUNNY) GALLIE
TYPESETTING BY DIATYPE SETTING CC, CAPE TOWN
REPRODUCTION BY POSITIVE IMAGE CC, CAPE TOWN
PRINTED AND BOUND BY TIEN WAH PRESS (PTE) LTD, SINGAPORE
AT NO GOVERNMENT EXPENSE

04 03 02 01 00 99 98   5 4 3 2 1

FOR PERMISSION TO REPRODUCE ANY OF THE ILLUSTRATIONS,
CORRESPOND DIRECTLY WITH THE ARTIST.
THE SMITHSONIAN INSTITUTION PRESS DOES NOT RETAIN
REPRODUCTION RIGHTS FOR THESE ILLUSTRATIONS INDIVIDUALLY
OR MAINTAIN A FILE OF ADDRESSES FOR PHOTO SOURCES.

CONTENTS

ACKNOWLEDGEMENTS

This book stemmed from our successful collaboration on *Elephants of Africa* which was published in 1986. During 1994 we followed this up with our second book, *The Magnificent Seven*, an account of the great tuskers of the Kruger National Park in South Africa. In the course of our travels across Africa in search of elephants in their varied habitats we also had many opportunities to observe other animals for which Africa is famous – and none proved more fascinating than the cats.

Our 'elephant travels' were not the beginning of our interest in Africa's cats, however, as we had always been intrigued by them – in fact, one of the first paintings that Paul ever sold was a portrait of a lion. Also, many of Paul's exquisite paintings and line drawings on cats were done years before he became particularly interested in the African elephant.

In gathering material for this book, we enjoyed the help and hospitality of our family, friends and colleagues – to all of them we offer our sincere thanks. We are particularly grateful for the support of our wives, Elaine Bosman and Catherina Hall-Martin, who contributed much to the genesis of this book, and for the encouragement and support of Kate, Simon and Christopher Bosman, Vega and Kate Hall-Martin – in many ways they gave us reasons for undertaking a project such as this. To Catherina our thanks are also due for typing a manuscript which seemed never to end.

Paul spent memorable times with Osric Bristow at his game ranch in Zimbabwe, in the process gaining wonderful insights into the ways and wiles of Africa's cats. Osric's untimely death was a great sadness, as he had done so much to make cats and other wildlife accessible for study. Joyce Bristow, and Viv and Carol Bristow have continued Osric's tradition and generously assisted when Paul needed reference material for his paintings. Anthony Gould is thanked for his footage of cats and Lucius Moolman for sharing with us his intimate knowledge of the caracal.

We thank Patrick Hamilton for providing us with information on the leopard and cheetah of Kenya; Dr Peter Norton for his reports on the leopards of the Cape mountains; and Professor J du P Bothma and Elias le Riche for making their work on the Kalahari leopards known to us before it was published. R H Daly, wildlife advisor to the Sultan of Oman, generously shared his recent reports of cheetah in that country with us.

We are grateful to Petri Viljoen, who is writing a doctoral thesis on the lions of Savuti in Botswana, for reading the manuscript and offering practical advice. We also thank Dr Michael Mills for offering his comments and ideas.

A book such as this derives much of its impact from the creativity and style of editors and designers. The team of Pieter Struik, Laura Milton and colleagues at Fernwood Press, and the inspired work of Peter Borchert and Willem Jordaan have added polish to our work. We thank them for their interest and inputs and their personal dedication to producing this book.

ANTHONY HALL-MARTIN   PAUL BOSMAN   SEPTEMBER 1997

As we approach the twenty-first century, the importance of conserving Africa's unique natural resources is greater than ever. Among these are no less than ten species of cat – part of the bounty with which this continent is blessed. But as Africa is developed, as economies and populations grow, as industry and the infrastructure which is part of modern life expands, the wild places which are the natural home of the cats, shrink and are transformed. Yet because of our knowledge of the plight of these animals the potential for conserving them is greater than ever. No species should now vanish into extinction, because we *do* know better than to let that happen.

This book, with its authoritative, scientifically accurate, yet easily readable text, complemented by delicate drawings and beautiful paintings aims to cultivate a clearer understanding of not only the biology of these animals, but also of the challenge of protecting Africa's cat species. It is to be hoped that it will also foster an appreciation of the wider African environment among its readers. Cats do not live in isolation – they are part of a complex and diverse ecosystem which this book also seeks to portray.

This is the first comprehensively illustrated work devoted to Africa's ten species of cat. CATS OF AFRICA is a significant addition to the literature of the continent's natural history, and to the objective of informing a wide readership of the status of its major group of mammalian predators. The book combines the knowledge and experience of a respected scientist, Dr Anthony Hall-Martin, with the skills, sensitivity and talent of an internationally renowned artist, Paul Bosman.

The importance of this publication will be appreciated and acknowledged, not only by all for whom the study and conservation of nature lie dear to the heart, but also by those who appreciate a beautiful book devoted to beautiful subjects. This book, it is hoped, will also contribute to fostering a wider desire for the ultimate survival of these magnificent animals.

A E RUPERT
PRESIDENT: WWF – SOUTH AFRICA

Most Westerners are probably familiar with pictures of Africa embracing flat-topped acacia trees, waving grasslands and herds of migrating wildebeest stretching across the horizon. This may be accurate of the Serengeti in Tanzania, but even then only for a brief part of the year – in fact, this image is far removed from the reality of what most of Africa looks like. The Serengeti-style picture is based more on the ease with which it can be filmed for television than on any real sense of how representative it may be of the wider African environment.

The same tendency to stereotype applies to people's perception of Africa's cats. For the most part, only the three larger members of the cat family are considered – a pride of lions lolling under an umbrella thorn, a leopard with its kill high in the branches of a jackalberry tree, and a cheetah staring out across the plains from the vantage of a termite mound . . . Quintessentially African

these images may be, but few people – even many of those with a fairly detailed knowledge of the continent's wild places – may know much about, or even have heard of the smaller cousins of these great cats that also form part of our unique natural heritage.

The reason why this should be so lies in part with the inherently secretive nature of cats, but it is also due to the sheer size of this ancient landmass. By any standards the continent of Africa is vast – it covers 30 million square kilometres. From north to south it extends for 8 000 kilometres and at its widest point it measures 7 500 kilometres across. The equator passes roughly through the middle of the continent, but a little more of the land lies to the north of it than to the south.

From the coastal plains the land rises to vast mountain ranges with peaks reaching more than 6 000 metres above sea level. Some mountains – ironically those on or near the equator – are snowcapped all year round. Over huge tracts in the central and equatorial regions, rainforests – or what remains of them – cover the landscape. Some of the mightiest rivers – the Nile, the Congo or Zaïre, the Niger and the Zambezi – cut through the African country-side. And there are deserts: the Namib in the south and the unimaginable wastes of the Sahara in the north. Temperate forests, grasslands, many types of woodland known widely as simply 'the bush', and the tiniest but arguably the richest of all plant kingdoms, the fynbos of the southern tip of the continent, all of these form part of the great mosaic of plant communities to be found in Africa. And in all of these places at least one species of cat finds its very own niche.

Africa is home to ten species of cats. They range from the diminutive black-footed cat, weighing just over a kilogram, to the majestic lion, weighing in at a mighty 250 kilograms. They are found in every major habitat and they are an integral part of every terrestrial ecosystem – on the plains, deserts and forests they are the ultimate predators, the animals at the very top of the pyramid of life.

Although varying in size, colouring and social behaviour, cats are suffi-ciently similar to indicate that they are fairly closely related, and are descended from some long-extinct common ancestor. In the light of these common anatomical features, taxonomists place them in one family, the *Felidae*, the clues to their close relationship lying in the anatomy of their skulls, as well as dentition, specialised feet armed with sharp claws, and supple muscular bodies. Carnivores all, they are designed for one purpose – to hunt and to kill.

Cats are largely nocturnal or crepuscular, preferring to hunt in poor light conditions, with only the cheetah and lion generally more active during the day. From time to time, however, most species can be spotted abroad during the day as well. Most of the African cats share similar social systems – they are solitary and territorial creatures, with adults generally consorting only at mating time. Only the lion and the cheetah are different – the lion living a social life in a pride, and the cheetah displaying a unique system in which males are social but females are not.

In Africa only the behaviour of lion and cheetah have been studied at length and in detail. The behaviour patterns of caracal, serval and leopard have been examined to a lesser degree, but the other five species remain little known. In the latter group, it is sad to reflect that more is known about dead cats than living ones.

Opposite: Discretion is the better part of valour – and a lion knows when to accept the indignity of a quick retreat.
Above: The security of wildebeest does not depend upon their speed of flight, but rather upon the alertness of herd members, and their ability to detect predators early.

The massive nests of sociable weavers accumulate over many seasons, and are a typical feature of the southwestern arid zone which stretches across South Africa, Botswana and Namibia.

With the exception of the lion, it is the habit of all African cats to mate and then go their own separate ways. The litter produced after a gestation period of somewhere around 70 days, depending upon the size of the cat, is rarely more than two or three. The young are known as kittens in the smaller cats, and cubs in the case of the lion, leopard and cheetah. All young are born in a helpless state and their eyes only open after about ten days. It takes a little longer before they are fully mobile.

Maternal care is good and cats are very protective of their young. There is far more social contact between youngsters in the cat species than there is among adults. This contact, in which play features prominently, serves to develop motor skills used in hunting, fighting and surviving. The young seldom remain with the mother for long and by the age of a year most are independent. All of the smaller cats of the subfamily *Felidae* can make a mewing sound, while the lion and leopard of the genus *Panthera* can roar. The cheetah, ever different, sole member of the genus *Acinonyx*, makes a range of birdlike chirping calls. All cats can snarl, drawing the lips back to expose the teeth and 'spit' in anger. Facial patterns, especially the lip colour, facial striping, and so forth, serve to emphasise the threat communicated by a snarl or growl, with the ears flattened. Most cats can purr – a vibrant sound usually related to contentment. Somewhat surprisingly – given the popularity of cats as household pets – scientists do not yet fully understand the mechanism by which the purr is produced.

The diet of a cat consists predominantly of the flesh of mammals, birds and reptiles. Other animals are also taken, especially by the smallest cats, but are usually of less importance than the first three groups. Vegetable matter is rarely eaten, although grass is often cropped – as a means of aiding digestion, rather than for its nutritive value.

As mentioned earlier, Africa's cats have carved niches for themselves throughout the varied African landscapes. It is easy to see this as some idyllic state that has persisted through the ages. Indeed the landscapes are ancient – the consequences of underlying geology and the forces of erosion, weathering, vulcanism, upliftment, folding and faulting which sculpted the land over aeons of geological time. These same processes created mountains, hills, escarpments, plateaus and valleys. By comparison, however, the patterns of vegetation we see today, with the attendant distribution of animals, is the result of only the past 5 000 years or so. Even this picture is of necessity only a general one, for the dynamics of vegetation communities such as the spread

Drainage lines and patches of moister habitat in African woodlands and savanna are often marked by water-loving Ilala palms.

of the Sahara into the Sahel and of the Karoo into formerly productive grasslands are now bringing about profound ecological changes to the continent.

Although change is an intrinsic dynamic of nature, the rate of change we are witnessing in Africa, and indeed the world, is not. The root cause of changes to the vegetation and the most dramatic wiping out of animal species yet experienced is the advent of modern man in his unstoppable, ungovernable numbers.

The growth in the human population and the expansion of cultivation and keeping of livestock have steadily eliminated wildlife by degrading the natural vegetation which supports it over much of Africa. In the rainforest, most larger animals are hunted for food and, as the 'bush meat' industry grows to satisfy the demands for meat and a cash income for a growing human population, wildlife stocks are being pushed into decline beyond the limits of sustainable harvests. Ultimately the threat of extermination looms over large areas.

As animals that provide the resource base for the survival of carnivores are eliminated, so numbers of predators decline. Over much of Africa the large cats have long since been wiped out – the lion is now only rarely found outside protected areas. The cheetah has disappeared from most of its former range and populations in even the most isolated areas of the Sahara are now under threat. Although leopards remain fairly abundant and widespread, their numbers are much reduced from what they must have been only a few decades ago.

The smaller African cats seem to be in no imminent danger of extinction, probably due to their highly secretive, nocturnal habits which generally ensure that they have very limited contact with humans. The only small cat that certainly is suffering is the African wild cat, whose population in the wild is being genetically swamped by inbreeding with domestic and feral cats.

One of the smaller cats that is not merely holding its own, but actually appears to be resurgent, is the beautiful caracal. But even here the explanation has a negative side, for this stocky, powerful feline is simply filling the niche left vacant by the elimination of leopards and black-backed jackals over much of southern Africa.

The conservation of cats, especially the larger ones, will always be fraught with difficulty and controversy. As with many other animals, their best hope must lie in national parks and other safari areas where the predominant form of land use is the sustained, rational use of the wildlife resource. Most African governments have committed themselves to conserving something of their natural heritage in national parks, but these sanctuaries can only survive on an evolutionary time scale if they are ecologically viable and if the wildlife populations are genetically viable. On this score, only a few of the larger parks can qualify. Therefore, there is still much to be done to make national parks viable, both ecologically and economically. Only then can we be reasonably confident that Africa's cats will survive with us.

Left: The grace of a leaping cheetah, perfectly balanced and deadly accurate.
Opposite: As with other cats, the charge of a cheetah is preceded by a careful stalk, with eyes riveted on the quarry.

Lean, lithe and agile, the cheetah is built for speed – a spotted cat with the body of a greyhound. It is the fastest mammal on earth. Every facet of its anatomy has been honed to serve one purpose – the chase.

It begins slowly, belying the electrifying explosion of energy that is to follow. From an elevated vantage point, which may be as much a device for observing the movements of prey as for watching for other cheetahs entering its territory, a likely looking prey animal is selected. Then, using whatever cover is available, the cheetah starts its approach – tense and purposeful, eyes riveted on its quarry – stopping instantaneously to stand motionless should the intended victim appear nervous.

Although the cheetah may lower its body during this initial stage of the hunt, it does not crawl on its belly like a leopard. Sometimes, however, the cheetah may not even bother to conceal itself and, with seeming nonchalance, may casually saunter towards its target across open ground.

Whatever the strategy of the day, the cheetah gets as close as possible to its prey before charging. The chase is unleashed by the prey taking flight. Movement is the trigger.

Seen in slow motion, with its extremely supple back alternately arching and stretching, a cheetah moving across the African veld at full speed is one of the most graceful sights in the world of nature. Back fully flexed, the hind legs reach well to the front of the forelimbs, straddling them as all four feet bunch beneath the body. Then, as the hind feet strike the ground one after the other in lightning succession, the body is powerfully catapulted forward. The spine unfurls, front legs reaching into the air and then down to the ground as the cheetah traces its incredibly long stride of up to nine metres.

I once witnessed a cheetah chasing an impala that was running very close to me. In watching the chase, it literally seemed to me as if the cat was flying behind the antelope, which stretched its stride to the utmost to escape. The impression of a flying cat is more than a mere illusion, though, as during more than half the length of its stride the animal is in fact airborne. All four of the cheetah's feet are off the ground simultaneously at least twice in each stride, once when the legs are extended and also when they are bunched together. The feet alternately hitting the ground seem to be doing no more than guiding the flying body.

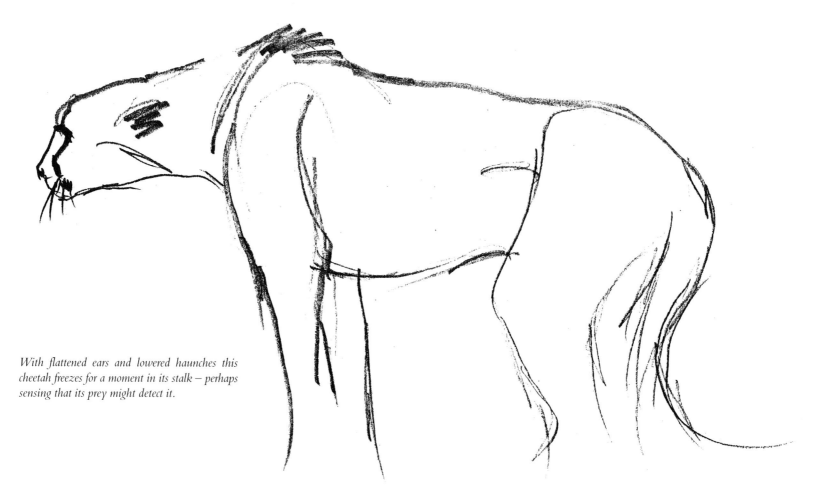

With flattened ears and lowered haunches this cheetah freezes for a moment in its stalk – perhaps sensing that its prey might detect it.

With its mouth half open, perhaps to help more air into the lungs, and ears flattened, the head is held level as if mounted on a gyro, eyes glued to the sprinting prey. If the quarry should turn or dart to the side the cheetah matches its every move, instantly changing direction even in mid stride, the heavy tail swishing across like a rudder to guide the body through the manoeuvre.

As the cheetah closes on its target it is forced to check its pace to avoid overshooting the animal now sharply twisting and turning in front. Such a miscalculation could be costly, allowing the prey to gain ground or even escape. But the cheetah is equal to the task, leaning into a turn with the entire length of its body at a very low angle to the ground and, when necessary, changing its leading foot in mid stride without losing any speed.

If the cheetah can draw level with its prey, a successful outcome to its chase is almost always assured. A forefoot armed with a razor-sharp dewclaw darts out to slap the shoulder, rump or thigh of the running antelope, inflicting a deep gash and knocking it off balance. Another useful technique is to hook a leg out from under the prey, tripping it into a spectacular high-speed somersault. As the animal falls, the cheetah's jaws snatch at its throat, clamping

shut for the life-sapping strangulation hold – the cheetah's usual method of dispatching larger prey. Young or smaller animals are killed by a suffocating bite gripping the muzzle, or by a precision bite to dislocate the vertebrae.

On film the chase and capture appear beautifully graceful, with every move quite clear. In reality the chase is a blur of speed. I once watched the final moments of a chase as a cheetah connected with a springbok in the dried-out bed of the Nossob River in the Kalahari. Both the animals were moving almost too fast for the human eye to follow and on impact they exploded in a cloud of dust, tumbling over and over, and coming to rest about 10 metres from the initial point of impact. As my eyes struggled to take in the scene I saw that the cheetah already had its jaws clamped high on the springbok's throat. The impact of the collision had been so severe that one of the antelope's horns had broken off.

As previously mentioned, the flight of the prey animal is the trigger which identifies the target and sets the cheetah off on its chase. If the animal does not run, the cheetah does not go after it. Cheetah at full stretch after a fleeing gazelle have been observed passing stationary territorial males that have not

Cheetah sauntering across open ground – a ploy which often brings them closer to alert gazelle who stand and watch as though mesmerised.

responded by running, while the cheetah sticks to its target animal, sometimes overtaking other prey animals in its dogged pursuit of the selected prey. Antelopes, or warthogs that stand their ground, therefore, are unlikely to be attacked, as the cheetah is apparently unable to knock over a standing animal as easily as a running animal.

The cheetah usually remains at right angles to the body of the animal that it grabs by the throat, thus keeping its vulnerable body well away from dangerous horns or flailing hooves. The cheetah may administer the killing bite while standing, sitting or lying next to the prey. When a mother with cubs is strangling prey the cubs may help by holding the struggling animal down with a bite to the flanks or by holding it with the paws. Antelopes may take anywhere from two to ten minutes to die, after which the cheetah releases its grip. If the animal struggles after the throathold is released, the cheetah will immediately grab it again and hold it by the throat for some minutes longer. The kill is usually dragged into the nearest shade or cover. The cheetah then rests, panting from the exertion of the chase and the kill, for up to thirty minutes before feeding. The degree of exertion is indicated by observations of the breathing rate of cheetah which may increase tenfold during and after a chase.

The need to get on with its meal is paramount, however, and once it begins feeding, it eats hurriedly, constantly glancing around for other predators or scavengers which so readily rob it of its kill. Cheetah usually finish feeding in one session and then move off – presumably to avoid contact with large scavenging competitors. There have been reports of cheetah scraping leaves and dirt over a kill in an attempt to hide the carcass, and then going off to fetch the cubs which immediately started feeding. More usually, however, the female takes her cubs on the hunt with her, concealing them when prey is spotted and inducing them, by vocal signals, to remain hidden while she stalks and kills an animal. If the hunt is brought to a successful conclusion nearby she then calls her offspring, who answer immediately and come running to the kill.

Cheetah cubs will usually start feeding immediately while the mother rests, if they are old enough to open the carcass themselves. If they cannot manage this on their own, she does it for them. Cheetah usually eat the thighs and buttocks of prey first, then the abdomen, rib cage and shoulders. They generally discard the intestines, but eat the heart and liver, also lapping up blood from the body cavity – probably an essential source of moisture in dry areas. Most of the articulated bones, the skin and head are left more or less intact at the end of a cheetah's meal.

Unlike the frenzied and highly aggressive behaviour shown by lions at a feed, a cheetah group sharing a kill is a most amicable affair. While some tussling for titbits may take place, there is no serious squabbling.

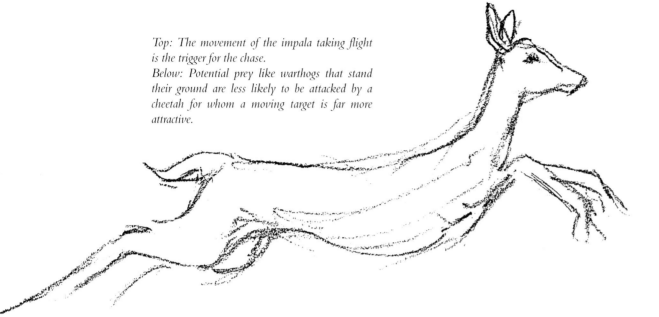

Top: The movement of the impala taking flight is the trigger for the chase.
Below: Potential prey like warthogs that stand their ground are less likely to be attacked by a cheetah for whom a moving target is far more attractive.

Many observers have recorded the cheetah's reluctance to defend its kill against other predators. Lions commonly rob cheetahs of their kills, as cheetahs will move off immediately at the sign of approaching lions. There are also numerous records of cheetahs being robbed by spotted hyaenas and leopards. It seems reasonable to suppose, therefore, that this retiring behaviour may be necessitated by the cheetah's vulnerability to injury. An injured cheetah that cannot hunt is likely to die of starvation.

✳

In contrast to the powerful and robust build of the lion and leopard, the cheetah, with its slender frame and long, elegant legs, seems almost fragile. Every aspect of its anatomy is crafted for speed and mobility – from its relatively small head and large, deep chest to its narrow waist and long tail.

The cheetah is commonly regarded as being unable to retract its claws, because they always remain exposed. In fact the claws *are* retractable, but, unlike other cats, cheetahs do not have the cutaneous sheaths which hide the claws – a characteristic which prompted many early writers to regard the cheetah as somewhat more closely related to dogs than to the cat family.

The head of the cheetah, being rounded and possessing a relatively short muzzle, gives it a somewhat flattened face, described by the writer Jonathan Kingdon as a necessary feature for an animal that depends upon using its

canines for strangulation of its prey. He bases his observation on the fact that while the cheetah's jaws remain clamped on its victim, the relatively high nasals are free of any breathing impediment as the cheetah pants to recover from the exertion of the chase.

The ears, too, are small and rounded and set on the sides of the head rather than on the top, as is the case in the serval and other cats. The size and location of the ears may be indicative of the fact that hearing, which is essential for the serval's hunting technique, is of little importance to the cheetah, which depends

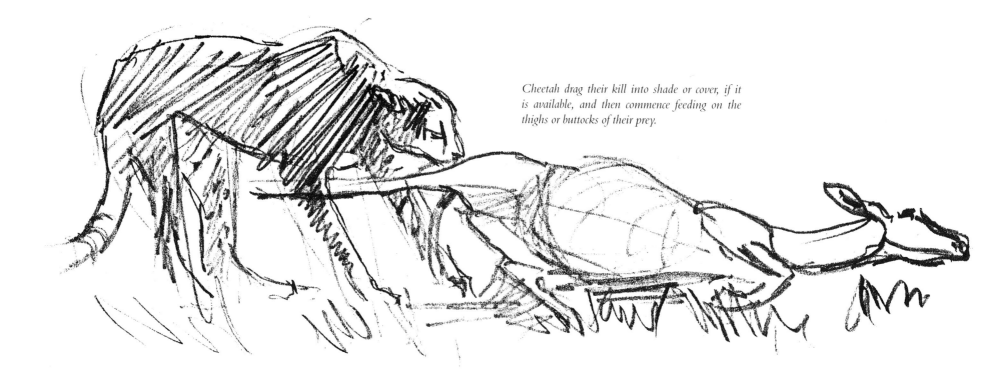

Cheetah drag their kill into shade or cover, if it is available, and then commence feeding on the thighs or buttocks of their prey.

upon eyesight. The eyes are, therefore, large, well-spaced and forward facing for good bifocal vision. The black orbits are outlined by white markings.

One of the cheetah's most clearly distinguishing features are its 'tear stripes'. This feature consists of two prominent black markings which start at the dark inner corner of the eye, run straight to about halfway down the side of the nose, then diverge in an outward curve on the sides of the muzzle, eventually joining the black upper lip. These stripes serve to enhance the cat's facial expressions, especially its snarl, during which the black outlines of the lips become a continuation of the tear stripes. There may be a considerable advantage to the cheetah having a fierce-looking snarl, as it depends largely on its snarling and posturing to intimidate a competitor, rather than on its ability to attack. The fanciful suggestion that the tear stripes exist as an anti-glare device does not seem plausible.

Apart from some variation, over most of its range in both Africa and Asia the coat colour of the cheetah appears fairly uniform, and most authorities agreed that there were no obvious colour or pattern differences upon which the cheetah of the two continents could be separated. The king cheetah of southern Africa, however, is very different.

The king cheetah was known to the local people of what was then Southern Rhodesia long before scientists ever dreamed of its existence. This legendary large cat was known as 'nsuifisi'. The local people described it as being neither a lion, nor a leopard nor a cheetah, but something totally different. It was first made known to the scientific world by a photograph of a skin and a letter from a Major A L Cooper, which was published in 1926 in the well-known British sportsman's magazine, *The Field*. Cooper suggested that the skin from near Macheke in present-day Zimbabwe was that of a hybrid between a leopard and a cheetah. Upon examination at the British Museum in London, the skin was recognised as a cheetah by R I Pocock, a noted mammal taxonomist of the time, but he described the animal as a new species to which he accorded the scientific name *Acinonyx rex*, the king cheetah.

The distinguishing feature of the king cheetah, or Mazoe leopard as it was also known – due to the area in which it was found – are its marvellous markings. Instead of the normal spotted coat of the cheetah, the king cheetah has large, black, free-form blotches on the flanks and hindquarters which coalesce into as many as five broad stripes running down its back to the base of its tail. In some individuals the stripes form a more or less solid black band from the shoulders to the top of the head. The legs have large, sometimes irregular, sometimes rounded, spots which extend down to the feet.

The belly and chest of the king cheetah is whitish to pale buff, and the throat and chin are white. The facial markings are similar to the normal cheetah, but the tear stripes are thicker, and usually some of the cheek spots are clustered together to form a distinct line running from the outer corner of the eye onto the cheek – much like that seen in the African wild cat and quite often in normal cheetah. The coat pattern of the king cheetah is highly variable and all known skins can be individually identified from each one's unique pattern. King cheetah also have longer, silkier fur than normal cheetah.

By 1980 there were records of no more than 13 skins of king cheetah known and 11 recorded sightings of live animals in the wild. Only a single photograph of a live animal, taken in the Kruger National Park in 1974, had ever been published. All the records of king cheetah came from a clearly circumscribed area of the southern savanna in Zimbabwe, eastern Botswana and the northern and eastern regions of South Africa. The concept of the king cheetah as a separate species had, however, long been abandoned and it was recognised as no more than an aberrant colour form of *Acinonyx jubatus*.

Then, in May 1981, a male king cheetah appeared in a litter of five cubs born to a normally spotted female at the De Wildt Cheetah Research Centre near Pretoria in South Africa. The centre had been hugely successful in breeding cheetah under the dedicated stewardship of Anne van Dyk, a pioneer of captive breeding of endangered carnivores in Africa. But this male was just the beginning of a surge in numbers of the king variety and over the following seven years a total of 14 kings were born from related De Wildt stock. Many more have been born since. Analysis of the pedigree of the kings and their parents confirmed that the coat pattern is determined by a recessive or unexpressed gene which must be carried by both parents.

In recent years wild king cheetah have regularly been seen in the Tshokwane area of the Kruger National Park and in the adjacent Mala Mala Game Reserve. The two Tshokwane kings were siblings in a litter of three in which the third sibling had the spotting of a normal cheetah. These two were seen for the first time as cubs in 1986 and were subsequently observed and photographed on several occasions. The Mala Mala animal, however, is regularly seen and its appearance and behaviour have been very well documented. The king gene is, therefore, safely conserved in the Kruger and adjoining cheetah populations.

Virtually all the other king cheetah localities reported are outside conserved areas where few cheetahs survive today. One must assume that they will in time be lost as those areas become more densely settled and the wildlife disappears.

Even when resting after a feed, a cheetah is alert, watching for enemies or rivals.

The rounded head, relatively short muzzle, small ears and prominent tear stripes down the sides of the face are characteristic of cheetah.

The Kruger National Park, Mala Mala and some of the larger ranches in southern Zimbabwe may eventually be the only reservoir of the king cheetah pattern in the wild, although the De Wildt population and a recently established population at Hoedspruit, will ensure that the genes are also preserved in captive populations.

The king cheetah has been described by Lena Bottriel as an incipient new species of cat, in the process of evolving. Insofar as the king is genetically determined, is localised within a specific area, and has appeared irregularly over many generations with fairly consistent characteristics, she has a case. The king cheetah could, in fact, be considered the very stuff of evolution if the pattern appeared at a higher frequency, and if there was a selective advantage to it. If, for instance, the kings enjoy a better rate of survival than the common pattern, then in time they may well become the only cheetah to occur locally. It could then be regarded as an incipient subspecies diverging from its parent stock. The common genotype, however, is still dominant within the cheetah population of the Kruger National Park, and as to whether a process of selection will take place, one can only guess. For the moment, there is no evidence that the king cheetah enjoys any selective advantage over the ordinary pattern in hunting, reproductive success or behaviour.

The cheetah has also been the subject of other instances of taxonomic confusion. In 1877 a new species of cat, *Felis lanea*, was described by P L Sclater. This was the so-called 'woolly cheetah' and the description was based on a live animal from Beaufort West in the Karoo region of South Africa. It had been caught as a cub and sold by a Mr Arthur Mosenthal to the Zoological Society of London. It lived at Regents Park for many years and when it died the skin and skull were deposited in the collection of the British Museum.

The woolly cheetah, like a few other aberrantly coloured animals mentioned in the literature, was unique. But of far greater interest than these isolated examples is the colour pattern of Adéle – the desert cheetah of the Sahara. It has never been adequately described and only recently were the first pictures of these mysterious cheetah published. The photographer, Alain Dragesco, spent three years in the Ténéré desert of Niger, which lies to the east of the Aïr Massif and far to the north of Lake Tchad. In this inhospitable region, where the rainfall is less than 100 millimetres in a good year and the desert is an inferno by day and freezing at night, he managed to take pictures of the sparse wildlife of the Sahara such as Dorcas gazelle, fennec, desert eagle owl, and the Sahara cheetah.

Adéle is the name used for the cheetah of the Sahara by the Touareg – the blue-veiled nomadic camel herders and warriors of the desert. No description of this spectacular animal has yet appeared in the scientific literature. The Sahara cheetah is a pale yellowish-sand to off-white colour with faint rusty, liver-coloured spots on the shoulders and flanks which darken to black on the back. In most individuals the familiar tear stripes on the face are entirely absent; in others there is a faint hint of darkening where one would expect the stripes to be. The rest of the face is plain with no hint of the spots and cheek stripe of other cheetahs. There are clustered dark spots on the top of the head – where the king cheetah is almost black. The spots on the flanks and on the back are arranged in orderly rows running the length of the animal from shoulder to pelvis. The tail has spots on it and these coalesce into several dark bands near the tip. The lower legs are whitish with no more than a few rust-coloured spots; the chest and throat are whitish-yellow.

In its colouring the pale Sahara cheetah vaguely resembles the woolly cheetah of the Karoo, and one needs very little imagination to picture the orderly rows of spots on the back coalescing into stripes. Could this be the origin of the king cheetah?

Adéle has survived into the last decade of the twentieth century, but there are only a few animals left. The chances of this spectacular cat ever being seen again by Western eyes, let alone photographed, are remote. Alain Dragesco has produced a monument to a cheetah which has never been seen by a scientist, and probably never will be. This cat will be gone before it has been properly described, and before the tantalising, desert-adapted behaviour which Dragesco observed has been studied.

✳

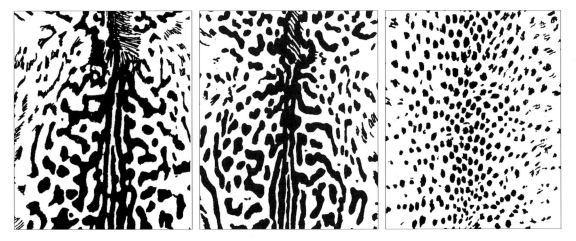

Above: Each king cheetah thus far recorded has a unique and recognisable coat pattern dominated by the extent of coalescence of the spots on its back. The convoluted and coalesced patterns of the king cheetah's coat (far left and centre) are very different to the discrete spots of the normal cheetah (left).

The Sahara cheetah are a pale washed-out sandy colour with faint spots and faded tear stripes.

Cats are characteristically nocturnal or at least more active at twilight than during the day. Cheetah also show activity peaks at around sunrise and sunset, but they are generally more active during the day than the other members of their family, and because they hunt by sight, this is not surprising. By being inactive at night they also reduce the chances of encounters with lions, leopard and spotted hyaenas, which generally act aggressively toward cheetah, robbing them of their kills and sometimes attacking them.

When cheetah make a kill late in the afternoon they will, if not disturbed, carry on feeding through the night, otherwise they rest. There are occasional reports of their hunting on moonlit nights, but except in the Sahara where they have perhaps adopted this strategy to escape the scorching daytime heat, this behaviour is unusual.

During cold weather, such as is experienced during winter in southern Africa, cheetah spend considerable time sunning themselves to warm up in the mornings. They also generally start to move around later on cold mornings than during warm weather. During the heat of the day they rest in shady spots. If they are territory holders they select an elevated position from where they can watch their surroundings. In the Sahara, where shelter is scarce, they have been found to rest in caves, under rock overhangs and even in underground burrows to escape the heat.

It is commonly believed that ideal cheetah habitat is open grassland. Certainly it is true that for a cursorial cat, hunting by sight alone, open country would seem more suitable. Most cheetah, however, occur in partially wooded or scrub-covered habitat and it seems that ideal cheetah habitat is determined more by prey abundance and lack of competition from other predators than by the vegetation. A balance between cover and visibility appears desirable, as cheetah seemingly enjoy greater hunting success in wooded country than on open plains.

The effects of competition with other large predators are not well understood. In arid areas, where cheetah tend to be more successful, there is less competition than in better-watered areas. However, it has clearly been shown in reintroduced populations in high-rainfall areas in South Africa where there are no lions and spotted hyaenas, and few if any leopard, that cheetah populations increase dramatically and soon have to be controlled.

The social system of the cheetah, which has only recently been adequately described, is unique among the cats. In fact, the cheetah's system of social males and solitary females is not found in any other species of mammal. Most adult male cheetah live in coalitions of two or three animals which form permanent social groupings. Adult females live alone, unless they have dependent cubs. Once the cubs are able to hunt for themselves, though, they leave their mother to go their own way.

Many past observers have noted that male cheetah litter mates remain together when they become independent of their mother. Dr Tim Caro, in his extensive study of the cheetahs of the Serengeti, has not only confirmed this, but has greatly expanded our understanding of the male coalition system. In total only 40 per cent of adult male cheetahs live alone. The rest live in groups: about 40 per cent remaining in coalitions of two, and 20 per cent forming threesomes. Furthermore, four out of five male groups consist of brothers, the balance comprising associations of unrelated males that have banded together. The long-term study in the Serengeti has shown that the male groups or coalitions are permanent and their members remain together for their entire lives – which may be as long as eight years.

The advantages to the male cheetah of living in groups can be explained by the size, quality and tenure of territories held by groups of males, as compared to single males. Singletons (comprising only some four per cent of the total) rarely managed to hold and defend a territory, whereas half of the two- and three-male coalitions managed to hold territories. Furthermore, when single males did manage to establish and defend a territory, they could only hold onto it for about four months. Against this record, pairs kept territories for eight months or longer, and three-male coalitions kept them for two years or more.

Dr Caro observed territorial males marking their 'properties' by spraying short bursts of urine towards the rear, or by defecating on prominent points. Marking was carried out at least once every hour. Non-territorial males did not show marking behaviour and they ranged over much larger areas than the territories of the settled males.

Whether in captivity or in the wild, cheetahs are avid scent markers. Males urinate on trees, bushes, rocks, termite mounds or other prominent points in their territories. They also climb on fallen or sloping trees, or trees with major branches close to the ground that they can easily clamber up, and then spray urinate. When patrolling their territories, they regularly visit the same spots and take great interest in sniffing at those points previously marked. Strange males also assiduously investigate such marking sites, which presumably indicate clearly who the occupants of the area are. Males may also deposit their faeces at marking stations in their territories. Defecation is then effected with a degree of ritual, as a small mound of earth may first be scraped together using the hind feet. The dung is then deposited on the mound. This presumably elevates the dung, making it more prominent, and distinguishes it from female droppings. Urine marking appears to be effective for about 24 hours, after which time its chemical message wears off. Female urine has no territorial significance. As the female approaches oestrus, though, her urine shows a high hormone content which attracts males.

It has been found that territories are centred around areas of high female population density, whether the females are present in the areas year-round, or only seasonally. Competition between males is therefore intense and there is only one way of settling the issue of territorial control – by fighting. The skirmishes (between individual males or separate male coalitions) are fierce and bloody, and contestants often suffer injury or death. The confrontations have seldom been observed, but judging by the injuries displayed by males and by the number of male carcasses recovered in the field, they take place frequently. The usual style of combat consists of flailing at the opponent with the paws and cutting with the dew-claw. Competitors also bite one another, and there is even one record of a vanquished male being suffocated by an adversary, just as a prey animal would be.

The adult sex ratio is heavily skewed toward females, and the mortality among males is so great that it has been suggested that only about half the males reaching adolescence ever survive to old age.

Having a partner as back-up in a fight makes the difference between keeping a territory – which offers mating opportunities – or losing it. Although the individual members of a male coalition share equally in any mating opportunities, the assurance that each will have some access to females and the chance of fathering cubs, seems a reasonable compromise. And since most members of male coalitions are brothers, with whom they share a complement of genes, it is no great loss to a male cheetah in an evolutionary sense to assist his brother to hold a territory and to mate successfully, as at least half of the same genes as his own are passed on to the next generation.

The relationship between male territories and female concentration areas in the Serengeti has been explained by the seasonal migration of Thomson's gazelle. These small antelope are almost exclusively the food resource of female cheetah. Male cheetah generally select larger prey species. The territories of females are, therefore, large enough to encompass both wet and dry season ranges of the gazelle. When the gazelle are more concentrated, the female

An adult female with her two grown cubs rest in a shady spot.

Right: Cheetahs' early morning wake-up rituals consist of sunning themselves and stretching.
Below: The uninvited guest appears – spotted hyaenas often rob cheetahs of their kill and are formidable competitors.

cheetahs' home ranges overlap considerably. In these smaller areas of concentration it is possible for male coalitions to hold relatively small territories that overlap with several females' ranges – thus giving the males access to more potential mating opportunities.

Male cheetahs that did not hold territories – mostly single males, but in some cases coalitions of males – were termed 'floaters' by the Caro research team. These animals travelled extensively and continuously, and were always found to be more alert and nervous than territory holders. Presumably, this cautious frame of mind is due to their constant avoidance of contact with territory holders who might kill them. The floaters, therefore, usually rested up in long grass or patches of concealing thicket rather than conspicuously out in the open on termite mounds or trees, as did territory holders. When the Serengeti cheetahs were examined closely for a radio-collaring project, it was found that most of the non-territorial males were in poor condition and suffering from some sort of infection or showing physiological signs of stress.

As mentioned previously, female cheetahs are solitary and occupy large home ranges, and much of the nature of their lifestyle is determined by whether or not they have dependent cubs.

Females have little contact with adult males. Courting and mating are brief encounters – sometimes lasting no longer than a day according to Caro – and are seldom observed. There is no further contact after mating and the male plays no part at all in raising the cheetah cubs.

Above: Lone cheetah males do not achieve nearly the same success at hunting or territory holding as those backed up by a companion.
Below: Cheetah have the ability to be completely relaxed while at the same time being totally alert and watchful.

Cheetah cubs are kept hidden in a den for five to six weeks after birth. It is crucial, therefore, that the mother chooses to have her cubs in an area where sufficient numbers of prey animals occur. If the gazelle leave the area, she is faced with the energy-sapping prospect of travelling long distances between hunting areas and the den, even though she can and does move the cubs from time to time. In some cases prey animals leaving a particular area has led to the mother abandoning her cubs. Cub mortality, as in the case of lion, is high. Approximately 80 per cent of all cheetah cubs born in the wild do not survive.

While lactating, the cheetah mother must hunt every day to satisfy her increased nutritional needs. Lactating females eat almost twice as much as non-lactating females. The increased hunting activity in itself is also more demanding of energy.

When the cubs are about six weeks old they are able to move around with their mother, but not yet able to hunt. During this period the female does not need to travel as far to hunt, as she can take her cubs with her. Her cubs remain vulnerable to other predators, however, and cannot yet outrun them. This means that she has to spend more time on the alert watching for predators, allowing her less time to rest. As the cubs grow older and become capable of assisting in the hunt, the demands on the mother lessen. For a few months the family hunts cooperatively, living and moving as a cohesive social group. Some time during the cubs' second year the family breaks up and the cubs – now young adults – move off as a group. The mother resumes her solitary life until her next litter is born.

Having shown that the members of sibling male coalitions are more successful at holding territories and therefore of ensuring access to mating opportunities, Tim Caro recently published his speculations on whether or not a cheetah mother was able to influence the potential success of her sons. His analysis offers some tantalising preliminary conclusions. For instance, cheetah mothers with pairs or trios of male cubs hunt more often each day than mothers with only one son, while data from forty females showed that such mothers did not rest after making a kill. Instead, after barely feeding themselves, they would set out once more to hunt for the benefit of their sons.

As the level of nutrition during growth is critical to development, it might be expected that better-fed cubs will be better developed physically than cubs getting a smaller ration of food (which is the case in litters with only one male or only females). Caro

weighed and measured a sample of nine male coalition members and eleven single males. He found that not only were the coalition members in better health, but that they were on average significantly larger and heavier than the singletons. This data provides a very strong indication that cheetah mothers with pairs or trios of sons are effectively, and differentially, helping them achieve an advantage against single males in the race for territories and mating opportunities. In this way a female possibly ensures that she leaves more descendants, which is the basic measure of biological success in natural systems.

When the female is not in oestrus she will usually behave aggressively toward approaching males. She may swat at the males while making a short rush or jump toward them and simultaneously uttering a staccato call. Males avoid contact and may vocalise in reply. Occasionally, and particularly when close to oestrus, the female allows the males close enough to sniff at her vulva. The testing male puckers his nose and grimaces in a flehmen-like sneer, much as ungulates do when testing the urine of a female. This may lead to some excitement on the part of the males, who then mock-charge the female. They also indulge in copious urine spraying. This behaviour, which is an integral part of territorial marking, is presumably elicited by the need or desire to keep strange males away, and in the context of mating it may be regarded as a ritual claim to the oestrous female. At this time the males also indulge in more frequent scraping up of mounds of earth onto which they urinate or defecate – an exaggerated form of advertising their territorial status.

During this period there is also a great deal of aggression between the individual members of the male coalition – presumably a jockeying for mating rights, even though the female is ultimately shared by the coalition members. Copulation in cheetah, in contrast to the lion, is infrequent. The female induces copulation by crouching down as a male approaches her from behind. The mounted male also effects a neck bite to the female, similar to that of the lion, but not with the same amount of growling and display of fangs. Copulation is rapidly completed. The peak oestrous period, during which there is close contact between males and a female, lasts only one to two days. After mating, the males and female go their separate ways with no further contact.

The gestation period is 90 to 95 days, after which a litter of between three and six cubs is born in a secluded den. The mother removes the fetal membranes from the cubs with her teeth and eats the afterbirth. The cubs are tiny, weighing only 250 to 300 grams each, and are blind and helpless like all kittens. As the cheetah female has five or six pairs of teats, she can

Left: Male cheetah who live together – providing essential back-up for each other during fights and while hunting – are usually brothers.
Opposite: Solitary male cheetah – also called 'floaters' – are almost constantly on the move to avoid territory holders who may kill them.

accommodate all her cubs during suckling. The site of the den is chosen for the protection it provides for the cubs, but the den usually consists of no more than a patch of flattened grass under a bush, a jumble of rocks or a densely vegetated gully or thicket. The Sahara cheetah has been known to use the underground burrows of tortoises, among others, as a nursery den.

Cheetah cubs are vulnerable to predators when they are small and still keeping to the den, as they cannot run away from their usual enemies – lions and hyaenas. There are many records of entire litters being killed and eaten while the mothers were away hunting, or after the mother had been driven

away from the den. There is even a record from the Kalahari of a brown hyaena killing an entire litter of cheetah cubs, and in the Kruger National Park a martial eagle was observed taking a cheetah cub.

Cubs' eyes only open after the tenth day. The eyes are dark-coloured while the cubs are young, gradually lightening as they grow older. The tear marks on the face are present from birth. The cubs can walk at three weeks and, as mentioned previously, they can follow their mother around by the age of six weeks. As the mother is dependent on food sources near her cubs' hiding place for the first few weeks, she may move them to a den closer to a concentration

Paul Bosman
77

of game, carrying them in her mouth, one by one, dangling by the scruff of the neck. When they are a little older she may shepherd them along by calling to them and guiding them, while continuing to keep a sharp look-out for other predators. There are many records of cheetah mothers moving their cubs around fairly frequently, apparently not only to get them closer to a concentration of game. There may be other reasons for vacating a den, such as the possibility of a den becoming flea-ridden, or to avoid predators that could be attracted to the den by the smell of the cubs, their urine or faeces.

Cheetah cubs are black at birth, thereafter gradually lightening and developing much longer, fluffier fur than their adult counterparts. Definition of spots appears gradually and up until about two months of age their spotting is so indistinct that they simply have a greyish appearance. They also have a mantle of long, smoky grey hair – up to eight centimetres long – on their backs. This mantle develops from about 14 days onward and helps to camouflage the cubs, especially when they are lying up in long grass or in the dappled shade of a thicket. Some writers have given credence to a fanciful theory that the cheetah cub's mantle is designed to make it look like a ratel or honey badger, which is notoriously aggressive, and in this way affords the relatively helpless cub some protection. By the age of about three months, when the cub is actively moving about with its mother, the mantle disappears, leaving only a slight ruff of longer hairs on the neck.

The weaning process starts at about six weeks of age, by which time the cubs have a full set of erupted milk teeth. The mother allows the cubs to tear and nibble at carcasses which she may drag or carry to some convenient place – usually a sheltered, shaded spot. By roughly three months of age the cubs are weaned, but they may still try to suckle up to about six months of age.

The average litter size of three to six cubs is greater than that of either lions or leopards, and the reason for this may well be found in the greater vulnerability of cheetah cubs to death by predation, veld fires and starvation. The cheetah mother must raise her large litter alone, unlike lionesses who have the assistance of the pride environment. Leopards, who also raise their cubs alone, usually have only one or two youngsters. Adult cheetah are also more vulnerable to predation than either lion or leopard and this may be a further factor favouring larger litters.

A cheetah mother will fiercely attack small predators, such as black-backed jackals, that approach her cubs and will also launch a determined charge at

Above: The fury of a cheetah cub is bluff, as it is virtually helpless.

spotted hyaenas or leopards. If her cubs are approached by a lion, however, the cheetah will make mock rushes, call and moan, but probably keep a safe distance between herself and the lion.

The cubs start taking an active part in the hunt at the age of about seven months. At this time the mother may sometimes assist the cubs in killing suitable prey, as though allowing them to practise. There have been several observations of cheetah mothers bringing a live animal to the cubs to kill. Mothers bringing Thomson's gazelle fawns and springbok lambs to their cubs have been recorded in East Africa and Etosha, respectively. This has been interpreted as the mother 'teaching' the young to hunt – it certainly gives the cubs an opportunity to learn hunting skills in a controlled environment. Similarly, a cheetah mother was observed placing herself between a warthog sow and her young, while her cubs did their best to catch the four squealing piglets. In play with their siblings young cheetah cubs direct their bites at the nape of the neck, the instinctive cat response, and presumably learn the stranglehold from watching their mothers kill.

Occasionally cheetah groom one another after a meal. Cubs and their mother may lick one another's faces, purring loudly all the while. This activity serves to clean the animals as well as to promote social contact. There is not, however, nearly the same degree of social grooming among cheetah that is found in a lion pride. Even the cheetah mother remains relatively aloof from close physical contact with her cubs.

Between the ages of about 12 and 15 months cheetah cubs may have acquired the skills to hunt, but may still need assistance from the mother with the kill. By about 16 to 18 months of age the cubs are almost fully grown, and they can survive on their own. At about this time the family breaks up with the cubs leaving as a group. The cubs may stay together until the females come into their first oestrus at 21 to 24 months of age, at which time the females strike out on their own.

The break between mother and cubs occurs abruptly, usually within the space of a few days – there is no gradual transition to independence. Once on their own, the cubs must fend for themselves and they usually manage this successfully, as there is no particularly high mortality at this time of their lives.

In the Serengeti, cheetah show a seasonal birth peak which appears to be correlated with that of the Thomson's gazelle, their main food source. In other areas of Africa there is less evidence of seasonality and cub sightings have been reported throughout the year in the Kalahari and the Kruger National Park.

Below and opposite: A sated cheetah – its belly clear evidence that it has had its fill – ignores the scavengers, such as white-backed vultures, which soon descend for a feed.

Left: An advantage of a social existence is that cheetahs can take turns at resting or staying alert and on guard.
Opposite: Like other cats cheetahs pant with open mouths when hot or after the exertion of an explosive chase.

In Etosha most births are recorded during the midsummer months. Some observers have suggested that cheetah births in East Africa are timed to avoid the periods when the dry grasslands are swept by fires which kill helpless cubs. As cheetah are polyoestrous a female losing her cubs may come into oestrus within two months and mate, though if her cubs survive she does not enter oestrus again until after they have become independent.

✳

Cheetah groups – such as a mother with grown cubs – may set off on a chase after a herd of animals, but each hunter appears to select its own target. Sometimes cheetahs take more than one antelope on such occasions, but usually the mother takes her target and the cubs hurry to help her restrain the prey or to kill it.

Cooperative hunting, which is not usually thought typical of cheetah, was regularly recorded in the South African lowveld when three captive-bred male cheetah were released into the wild. They had not been taught to hunt by their mother, and so they attacked prey such as giraffe and buffalo which would normally be ignored. They only went after giraffe if there was a youngster

among the herd, however. One cheetah would get the herd running, while the other two attacked the calf. One of these would hook a dew-claw into the rump of the giraffe calf and pull downward while the other hit the calf high on the shoulder. The combined efforts of the two cheetah would knock the giraffe to the ground. The cheetah that attacked on the shoulder would then deliver the strangulation bite high on the throat. In four out of five witnessed giraffe kills, the same cheetah performed the same function each time. This cooperative hunting was seen only when the target was a giraffe, or on one occasion with a waterbuck, which is a much larger animal than a cheetah. When hunting more usual prey, the size of impala or duiker, there was no cooperation between the three males at all.

In East Africa Jonathan Kingdon has noted that it is not unusual for several cheetah acting together to take large prey. The Sahara cheetah have also been observed taking part in cooperative hunting, as in their case a failed hunt obviously has far more serious consequences.

Although cheetah lack the power to take very large prey animals, they are known to have wide-ranging tastes. Generally, however, they concentrate on small to medium-sized antelope or the young of larger species. In both Asia and Africa gazelle are particularly sought after. For a cheetah an ideal prey animal usually weighs less than 30 kilograms.

Cheetah generally select younger animals if they are available. These fawns or lambs provide only a small meal, but they are obtained with little effort. Toward the end of gestation, when she is heavily pregnant, a female cheetah may not be able to run fast enough to catch an adult antelope. At this time she concentrates on hares and lambs which are easier to catch. Records show that among their adult prey items they also select for females rather than males, and are more successful at taking very old animals. Even so, the bulk of their prey items are in good condition and they do not necessarily select weak animals.

Cheetah have also been recorded killing, and occasionally eating, other carnivores like black-backed jackal, bat-eared fox and, on rare occasions, others of their own species.

It is difficult to arrive at a figure of how many prey animals are killed by a single cheetah in a year. This varies according to the condition, age and sex of the cheetah, for example whether it is a female with cubs to feed. George Schaller monitored a female cheetah with two young cubs for 26 days in the Serengeti. During this period she killed 24 Thomson's gazelle and a hare.

Below: For the first three months of its life a cheetah cub has a ruff or mantle of long, smoky grey hair on the neck and shoulders.
Opposite: Using the available cover, two cheetah scan the area for prey – cooperative hunting is one of the features of male cheetah groups.

Right and opposite: Cheetah sometimes sit on their haunches staring, seemingly vacantly, into the distance. They are more likely to be focusing on potential prey, however, and sizing up their chances of a successful stalk or chase. The flashing white wing feathers of an alarmed male ostrich, in addition to movement, is the spur to attack. A singled-out bird is followed until contact is made, the cheetah usually grabbing the bird by the wing whilst taking care to avoid the thrashing legs which, armed with a vicious toenail, could easily disembowel a predator. After subduing the ostrich the cheetah seizes the vulnerable throat, and the bird is suffocated.

Other observations on the same animal took the total monitoring time to 35 days, during which the cheetah had killed 31 gazelle and the hare. Sometimes a day or two would pass without her making a kill, but at other times she killed two gazelle in one day. The overall kill rate works out to about 341 gazelle a year for a female cheetah with cubs.

Data from Kenya showed a solitary cheetah killing every two to three days, or at least 150 gazelle a year. Groups of cheetah making larger kills spend more time feeding on the carcass and kill at greater intervals. Similar data was derived from studies on cheetah in the Kalahari. The daily food consumption of wild, adult cheetah under different conditions has been estimated at from about two to four kilograms a day. Cheetah, like other cats, can gorge themselves on a kill and then go for several days without eating.

Hunting success varies from about 10 per cent of chases ending in success to 70 per cent, depending on the prey species being hunted and the conditions of the hunt. Generally adult female cheetah with cubs are the most successful hunters. This may be because they are more careful about selecting and approaching prey, as they have more to lose in the event of a failed hunt. The vulnerability of the prey and the degree of cooperation between hunting cheetah also contribute to the failure or success of the hunt. A study has shown that three captive-bred male cheetah released into the wild did not cooperate when the prey was impala, and between them could only record a 10 per cent success rate. When the prey was giraffe, however, and the three hunters worked together, their success rate rose to 40 per cent.

Cheetah drink at irregular intervals, even when water is available. In the

Kalahari they can go without drinking for long periods of time. Cheetah obtain much of their moisture requirements from their prey and there are many records of cheetah lapping up blood from the prey's body cavity. In the Kalahari, Willie Labuschagne has recorded cheetah eating tsamma melons, which are a major source of water for most ungulates in that environment.

Cheetah do not normally eat carrion and although there are a few records of their eating animals that they have not killed themselves, those that they did eat were usually taken when still fresh.

✳

Once cheetah populations were widespread through-out sub-Saharan Africa. They occupied virtually all woodland, savanna and shrub-savanna areas, including the arid rangelands of the Karoo in the south, and were found deep into the Sahara in the north. From Africa's western deserts, through Libya, Egypt, the Middle East and Arabia, to India and what are now the states of Pakistan and Bangladesh, the cheetah lived and hunted. Only rainforests were not suited to its lifestyle.

Sadly, the range of the cheetah in the closing years of the twentieth century is no more than a reminder of what it was.

In Africa, viable and healthy populations are now largely confined to protected areas such as national parks, with most of the cheetah still found beyond the borders of these sanctuaries having been reduced to remnant groups. Elsewhere, the cheetah has been even less successful. It became extinct in India by 1952 and it is now very rare anywhere in its Asian range, while on the Arabian Peninsula there have been only about half a dozen reliable reports of cheetah sightings since 1950.

Over the centuries there have been many instances of cheetah being tamed and kept for sport hunting, and even today, where laws allow such aberrations, there are instances of these beautiful spotted cats being kept as pets. Possibly the oldest record of man using cheetah is a silver vase decorated with a representation of a cheetah wearing a collar. It was unearthed at Maikop in the Caucasus from a burial mound dated 2300 BC.

Although most of the records of cheetah being used for hunting and adornment come from the Middle East and Asia, it also occurred in Europe. There are accounts of cheetah coursing in Italy as early as the fifth century AD. Cheetah coursing in England was a rarity, but there is a record of a cheetah

having been presented to George III. Jonathan Kingdon refers to this in his book on the hunter, as well as the disappointment of the assembled nobility at Woodstock Park where the cat was released after a red deer. The stag did not run, instead turning on the cheetah and tossing it high into the air. Thus deterred, the cheetah refused to hunt again. No wonder – the red deer weighs 100 to 120 kilograms – far beyond the range of prey which would normally be attacked by cheetah.

Even though the Moghul emperor, Akbar the Great, reputedly kept up to 1 000 cheetah, it is unlikely that such actions ever had any serious impact on the animal's numbers. Instead, as is almost inevitably the case, it has been the increase in human numbers and the proliferation of domestic animals that have taken their toll. The cheetah, like the lion, has found coexistence with modern man and his livestock impossible. Thus, as human populations have spread and tamed the environment, the cheetah's numbers have declined and its range has shrunk.

During the middle decades of the twentieth century the fur trade may also have contributed to worsening the cheetah's plight in some areas. On the other hand, this trade at least ensured that cheetah had a commercial value – cattle ranchers in Namibia and Zimbabwe, for instance, could tolerate the loss of a few calves now and again providing they could recoup their losses from the sale of cheetah skins. Once Western conservationists achieved a ban on the trade in skins of spotted cats, the species became worthless to ranchers as there was no longer any hope of making good their losses. From then on cheetah have been regarded as useless vermin. Consequently, more have been shot since the ban, and their numbers are declining even faster. In Namibia alone the cheetah has declined from an estimated population of 4 000 to 6 000 at the height of the spotted fur trade to roughly 2 500 animals in 1996.

In the Sahel the cheetah is hunted as a killer of livestock such as goats and camels. The livestock also compete with the desert wildlife for grazing, thus reducing the available supply of prey for the cats, and so steadily wearing down the last populations of the Sahara cheetah.

It is too much to hope for at any stage in the future that cheetah could survive anywhere in Africa outside of national parks. This is already the case in most parts of southern and West Africa, and it serves to underline the value of these constitutionally protected sanctuaries. It may appear unpalatable to the sensitivities of some, but if Western conservationists could be persuaded to harness their efforts to promote national parks rather than counterproductive trade bans, they would achieve a lot more for the cheetah and its long-term survival.

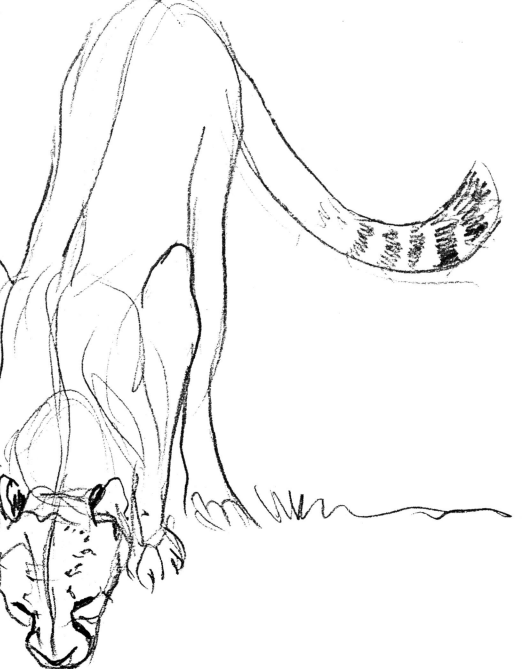

Opposite: Male cheetah often make use of fallen or sloping trees to act as terrorial beacons on which to spray, urinate or defecate to advertise their presence to rivals.
Below: Cheetah in the Kalahari derive most of their moisture needs from their prey, but drink from time to time during the rains when free water is available.

Right, and opposite: African myths often portray the elusive leopard as guileful, cunning and strong. These characteristics may explain why it is the most widely distributed large predator on earth.

The leopard is an animal of great beauty – the perfect example of feline power and grace. Solitary, secretive and aloof, it is an unmatched predator, and a powerful symbol of the wild places of the earth. To see a leopard moving through the African bush, or even lying motionless draped in the high branches of a tall tree, is a riveting experience. But to witness the sinuous power of the animal as it takes prey its own size or even bigger is a moment indelibly imprinted on mind and eye – a blur of hunter and hunted tumbling in the dust. Almost before the moment can be comprehended it is over – the cat's jaws tightly clamped around the victim's throat as its life slowly ebbs.

The speed and focused fury of a leopard attack is bewildering. But behind it is a seemingly choreographed moment of poise and majesty that only the technique and skill of wildlife photographers can truly capture. One particular sequence filmed recently at the Mala Mala Game Reserve in South Africa revealed this more vividly than I can ever recall seeing before. The young leopard, only recently forced by her mother to fend for herself, needed to make a kill. Her hunting technique lacked the consummate ability and confidence of a more mature animal, but determination and a measure of desperation drove her on. The camera crew, equally determined to follow her fortunes and to film her first success, tracked her as best they could.

Whilst cautiously making her way through the woodland undergrowth, the leopard came upon a small herd of impala, but not cautiously enough, and in a moment the skittish antelope were dodging and leaping through the bush in a flurry of hooves and tawny flanks, presenting an impossible confusion of targets for the young, inexperienced hunter. As luck would have it, however, a fully grown male came charging out of the gloom straight towards her. In

ing them in such densely vegetated parts, we do know that it is a rich environment for the leopard. Although ungulate biomass is limited to the various species of forest duiker, the royal antelope, chevrotain, bushbuck, bongo, bushpig and giant forest hog, the leopard's menu is bolstered by the considerable number, and variety, of primates and arboreal rodents, as well as abundant birds, reptiles and fish.

A highly significant aspect of the leopard's success in rainforest habitat is that competition with other large predators is minimal, as lions and hyaenas are absent. The African golden cat and other forest carnivores such as genets are much smaller than the leopard, and not likely to offer a serious challenge in the food stakes. Also, as a solitary and stealthy hunter, equally at ease operating by night or day, and an expert climber to boot, the leopard is well suited to exploiting the forest environment.

Although leopard densities in savanna and woodland are generally much lower, they can reach high levels where bands of riverine forest or thicket abut more open woodland, or cut across grassland and open savanna. Such areas are rich in the 'right-sized' prey species for leopards – bushbuck, impala and other small to medium-sized antelope.

Some of the more unusual habitats occupied by leopards in Africa include the sparsely vegetated sand dunes of the Kalahari Desert, a frequently waterless expanse where it relies, like lions and cheetahs, on the moisture derived from the blood and body fluids of its prey, as well as the tsamma melon, which has a high water content. Also, as much as the leopard is popularly associated with the summer-rainfall savanna, it is found in the mountain ranges of the Western Cape in South Africa where the rains come in winter and the vegetation is a dense macchia with scattered forested ravines. Here it often snows in winter, but this is no impediment to an animal that is able to survive the ice and snow of the High Atlas of Morocco and the almost alpine conditions of the Ruwenzoris, Virungas, Mount Kenya and Mount Kilimanjaro, at altitudes as high as 4 000 metres above sea level. The only abundant mammalian prey at these levels are rodents and hyraxes – adequate fare for leopards.

✳

Casually draped over a branch in a convenient tree, a leopard simultaneously keeps cool, relaxes and watches for potential prey.

Above and opposite: Leopards are highly selective of their daytime resting sites, preferring elevated vantage points from where they can view the surrounding countryside and potential prey.

The call of the leopard does not match the thunder of a male lion in full voice, but once heard it is a sound as unforgettable as any in the chorus of the African night – a hard, grunting, rasping sound likened to the sawing of wood. I would suggest, however, that the full impact of a leopard's rumbling growl is every bit as terrifying as that of its larger relative. This is especially so when it is hurtling towards you in a charge, or when one is approaching a trapped or cornered animal, as I have had to do on a number of occasions.

Adult males genraly call to advertise their territories. When a female calls, it is frequently as she approaches oestrus when she possibly does so to attract a potential mate. Even to the human ear individual leopards have distinctive calls, and for several years I kept track of a leopard who regularly patrolled the streets of Skukuza, headquarters of the Kruger National Park, where I lived for many years. It is more than likely, therefore, that leopards can also distin-guish the voices of their fellows.

Recognizing one another from a distance must have distinct advantages for leopards as they are solitary beasts and adults generally avoid one another, with the exception of the brief encounters to mate or to defend a territory. Usually they are active during the night and at twilight, when they prowl their territories, hunting if they are hungry or if the the opportunity presents

the drama of slow motion that is part of the modern film-maker's repertoire, the leopard uncoiled out of the grass to meet her quarry. At the moment of impact, both animals were at least a metre off the ground, the force of the collision cartwheeling them through the air in a balletic arc. As they hit the earth, the leopard's jaws had somehow found their target, but still, the powerful male impala managed to struggle on and victory for the cat seemed far from assured. Within a few paces, however, the antelope faltered and minutes later the leopard, chest still heaving, lay triumphantly by her first successful kill.

I have been privy to many moments of high drama in the bush, and like most of us with a penchant for such things, I have witnessed many more, albeit vicariously, on video and film. For me, however, the scene just described was unlike any other, a true celebration of both the cameraman's skill and uncanny anticipation, and the supreme athleticism and courage of the leopard.

The leopard is the most widely distributed and successful of the world's large cats; it occupies more diverse habitats than any other mammal save man and a few commensal rodents. It holds its own in rainforest, frigid mountains and burning deserts – a range extending 16 000 kilometres and more from Mauritania in the west, clear across Africa, Arabia and Asia to Manchuria and Siberia in the east. The leopard is found as far north as latitude 50° in far eastern Russia, while to the south it prowls the coastal mountains of the Cape of Good Hope. In all kinds of vegetation, the leopard makes a living. It alone among the large cats can survive, and even thrive, close to human habitation. The only parts of Africa uninhabited by leopards in recent times are the most extreme and lifeless areas of the Sahara and Namib deserts.

The key to this wide habitat tolerance lies in the ability of leopards to carve niches for themselves almost anywhere, and especially with respect to their catholic taste in food. Birds, snakes, rodents and other small mammals, virtually all the antelopes, wild sheep and goats, as well as livestock are included in the diet of these remarkable cats.

Although leopards are successful in rocky and bushy habitat, they occur mostly in areas of taller vegetation where, in the canopy of sturdy trees, these secretive cats spend much of their time. It is, however, in the rainforests of Africa and Asia that leopards are reputed to reach their highest density. Certainly, if leopard numbers per unit area is the criterion of habitat suitability, then the forest is by far the leopard's optimum habitat.

Notwithstanding that our knowledge of animals in the African rainforest is limited, to some degree because of the obvious difficulties associated with count-

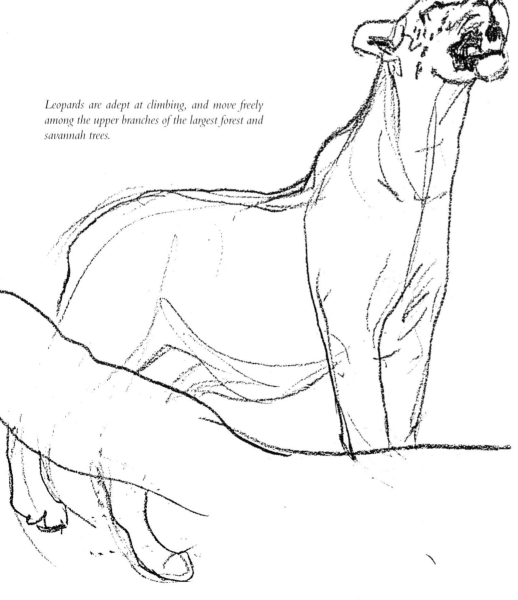

Leopards are adept at climbing, and move freely among the upper branches of the largest forest and savannah trees.

Opposite: In the savannas of southern Africa leopards are commonly found on granite outcrops, resting in the shade of evergreen trees such as figs. Right: Africa's massive baobabs often act as small ecosystems, providing food, water, roosting sites for bats and birds, and resting sites for leopards.

itself. Otherwise they spend the time patrolling and scent-marking. During the day leopards will rest up in some secluded spot – a tangled thicket, a shaded ledge among a jumbled mass of boulders, or on a conveniently wooded termite mound. The most characteristic resting place, however, is high in the branches of a large tree, the thick-branched marula being a favourite in the southern African bushveld, as are the sausage tree and the leadwood.

In the Meru area of Kenya, on the other hand, leopards are most often seen in the umbrella thorn, which is the most common large tree, while in the Tsavo National Park, favourite resting places are baobab trees and certain members of the mahogany family.

That leopards are discriminating in their choice of a resting site is apparent from my own sightings as well as from the more detailed studies of Patrick Hamilton in the semi-arid Tsavo National Park of Kenya. Hamilton found seasonal differences in leopards' use of rock outcrops or trees. During the dry season, when the predominantly deciduous trees and shrubs of the savanna had lost their leaves, these cats showed a significant preference for lying up on hills or rocky outcrops. Here caves, overhangs and densely clustered evergreen trees and shrubs create deep shade for concealment, as well as safety and good vantage points. During the rainy season, however, when savanna trees are in full leaf, leopards are more frequently found in their lofty boughs.

In the Kalahari Desert, where large trees are scarce, the leopard usually selects a densely leaved evergreen shepherd's tree as its resting site. These trees are usually low-growing in the Kalahari with a skirt of branches that almost touch the sand, thereby creating deeply shaded, sheltered lairs that are also favoured by lions and cheetahs. By far the most popular of male leopard resting sites identified by researchers in the Kalahari have been shepherd's trees, others being the ubiquitous camel thorn and low-growing thorny and dense shrubs of blackthorn.

Right, and opposite: During the dry season in the southern savanna game like impala, blue wildebeest and warthogs cautiously congregate at water holes or in riverbeds, knowing that any large trees nearby could conceal a leopard in ambush.

Vegetation is not the only choice of refuge, however; over 20 per cent of male leopard resting sites and half the sites chosen by females with cubs in the Kalahari were the underground burrows of aardvarks and porcupines. These earthy hide-outs provide the major physiological requirements of shade and cover, but obviously do not constitute vantage points for keeping an eye out for prey or potential danger.

Leopards are expert tree-climbers and have no trouble getting up a tree or descending, head first, to the ground. Their unsheathed claws gain purchase on even the smoothest bark. They are very much at ease aloft and move with confidence along swaying branches high above the ground. It is no surprise, therefore, to find that leopards in forest environments are adept at catching monkeys and other primates.

It is when climbing trees that the leopard's great strength is most clearly demonstrated, as, even when gripping prey exceeding its own body weight, it can scale near vertical trunks with consummate ease. Occasionally, climbing up into the tree tops may be more than a means of seeking a cooling breeze, concealing prey, or simply an expression of their forest origins. As leopards generally choose positions from where they can see without being seen, it is likely that the great value of their elevated resting spot is its function as an observation post – not only as might seem obvious, to pounce on or to watch for prey, but possibly even more importantly, to avoid the attentions of lions and spotted hyaenas, not to mention their most dangerous competitor, another leopard.

The value of the leopard's spotted pelage as camouflage is wonderfully demonstrated when it is lying in dappled shade – its lithe body hugs the branch

so that there is no sign of a giveaway silhouette, while the variegated pattern of sunlight and shadow falling on the coat complement its broken design.

✳

The solitary life of the leopard is well documented — the general exceptions to this singular lifestyle being the relatively short association of a female and her maturing offspring and the even briefer alliance of adult male and an oestrous female. Recent observations in the Mala Mala Game Reserve in the lowveld savanna of South Africa, however, showed a male and female in regular contact throughout the period that she raised their cubs — but this appears to be unusual. For the rest, they walk alone.

Males occupy large territories which they aggressively defend against other

males, although they occasionally tolerate overlapping boundaries. Some unique footage in the recently released documentary film *Beauty and the Beasts*, made in Mala Mala, shows two adult males pacing along parallel to each other, a few metres apart, each guarding the boundary of his territory. Females, on the other hand, live in home ranges which may partly overlap the territories of several males. Male territories are usually much larger than female ranges and may overlap several female ranges, thereby ensuring maximum mating opportunities for both the males and females.

In valuable tracking studies carried out in the Tsavo National Park on leopards fitted with radio collars, Patrick Hamilton showed how the territorial boundaries of male leopards form a space-efficient mosaic with very little overlap. He was also able to gather data indicating that fighting among male leopards was fairly common and severe, despite a repertoire of other actions designed to keep interlopers out of an occupied territory. These avoidance tactics varied from scent marking, tree scratching, depositing faeces where other leopards would find them, and calling to warn rivals away.

Leopards regularly use scratching trees which they visit during the course of their territorial patrols. I often watched a large male leopard near Skukuza – easily distinguished from a female by its heavy-jowled profile – following the same route between the Sabie and Sand rivers, and visiting the same trees. Often such trees are on a boundary of a particular male's territory and have a large branch spreading horizontally fairly low down, or the trees themselves may have sloping trunks. A leopard visiting such a tree first sniffs carefully at its base before leaping up onto the scratching branch. Here, too, it stretches out, sniffing at existing scent marks before scratching with its forepaws, or it crouches, scratching backward with its hind feet. It may also loll on the branch, rubbing its chest, cheeks or perineal region on the bark.

Although it has yet to be established, it is generally presumed that leopards have scent glands on their paws which leave chemical messages for other leopards. It is also a common leopard practice to spray urine in prominent places, including branches or scratching

Opposite: The dappled effect of the light falling on a leopard's coat, the contours of the branches, and the variegated pattern of the bark combine to camouflage the cat. Right: Leopards use branches or scratching trees for territorial marking.

trees, as another means of chemical communication. Urine spraying is done by both males and females. Leopards are also known to enjoy rolling on bare patches of ground, in elephant dung, on old carcasses and even on oily patches on tarred roads, and it has been speculated that there may also be an element of olfactory communication involved in such behaviour.

In areas with a high density of leopards, such as where prey is abundant, male territories may overlap to a considerable degree. For example, two adult males in Hamilton's study area had territories which overlapped by as much as 70 per cent, but the area was uneasily shared. Despite the overlap, his data showed that these two males actively avoided contact, maintaining an average distance between them of about three kilometres. By concentrating their activities in different parts of their ranges, they ensured separation in time and space, illustrating that common use of the area did not imply simultaneous use.

Studies on male leopards in the Cedarberg range in the Western Cape by Peter Norton, a colleague of ours, showed a similar mosaic of territories occupied by adult males. Two particular males had an overlap of as much as 57 per cent. The data showed, however, that as one prime male slowly expanded the degree of overlap into the territory of an old male, the other animal correspondingly shifted his centre of activity further away from the encroaching rival. Eventually the old male moved out of his original territory and was killed by a farmer. He was in poor condition and his canine teeth were broken, indicating that he was probably not able to defend himself effectively against the younger, stronger male.

In addition to regular movements around their territories, male leopards, like many other carnivores, have been found making irregular

studies have shown that whereas a male leopard in the prey-rich Chitwan jungle of Nepal can live quite comfortably in eight square kilometres, a leopard in the Kalahari Desert needs up to 400 square kilometres to meet its food requirements. Consequently, leopard densities are low where large territories are required and high in habitats where small territories are adequate.

✳

Female leopards approaching oestrus attract the attention of males by calling, as well as by leaving olfactory clues on trees and bushes. These signs include hormones voided in urine and possibly also secretions of the anal glands. Females also drag their hind legs and scrape the ground, thus leaving telltale physical signs lasting six to seven days. Furthermore, with oestrus imminent, females become more restless, wandering to the farthest boundaries of their ranges and beyond. It is not unusual for a female to leave her normal range for a few days, and to stay in the company of an escorting male when she is ready to mate. If she does not meet up with a male, mate and conceive, she returns to an oestrous state about 45 days later.

Little is known about leopard courtship in the wild. At Mala Mala and Londolozi, however, matings have often been seen and occasionally filmed and photographed. My own observations are limited to one brief episode witnessed in Malawi. There was much growling, hissing, snarling and calling – which made the event sound more like war than

forays abroad into areas occupied by competitors and then returning 'home'. These expeditions may be to test the determination of a neighbour's defence, or to seek oestrous females.

The daily movements of a male leopard are correlated to the size of his territory. Animals occupying large territories have a lot more patrolling to do and may move twice the daily distance of an occupant of a small territory. This extra movement has an energy cost which must be met by more frequent or larger kills. Generally, average daily distances travelled are only two to five kilometres, indicating that leopards are fairly sedentary animals. In the Tsavo National Park, however, their forays away from their home territories took them up to 11 kilometres afield. In the Stellenbosch mountains near Cape Town, where leopards are free to roam over large areas and the habitat is less suitable, the daily distances travelled are more than twice as great as in Tsavo, and the territories are many times larger.

The variation in territory size is clearly a function of available food supply: the less food, the larger the territory. Radio tracking and other like love – but the vocalizations ended abruptly after mating. As with the other cats, the female crouched down in front of the male several times before he mounted her, rumbling and growling all the while. At the end of mating the male gave a 'love bite' to the female's neck, much in the manner of lions and cheetahs, and then sprang away as the female turned to swat at him with a forepaw. Occasionally more than one male has been recorded following an oestrous female, and males fighting over an oestrous female have also been seen. Mating is brief, accomplished at night or by day, and repeated several times with the same male or different males – often with matings being as little as five minutes apart.

Gestation lasts from 90 to 100 days and the cubs are born in a carefully selected shelter among rocks, under a rock overhang, in a cave or dense thicket, or even down an aardvark burrow. The usual litter size is two or three, but it is rare for more than one or two to survive to independence. Each newborn cub or kitten weighs about 450 grams, and is blind and helpless. The fur of leopard cubs is much longer and darker than that of older animals, and the spotting is indistinct. By eight to ten days, however, the dark, slate-grey eyes open, and the cubs begin to take an interest in their surroundings.

During the first few weeks of their lives the cubs are kept well hidden. Crevices in rock outcrops, or lairs which are far too small for the mother herself to enter, are often used for this purpose. A den I examined along the Sweni River in the Kruger National Park, was a space of no more than 20 centimetres high, between two layers of granite boulders on a small outcrop. In the mother's absence the cubs retired to the darkest recesses of this little cave. On her return she was seen coaxing them out, making low panting calls to bring them to her to suckle and to be groomed. She also moved them to a new hiding place every few days, carrying them one at a time in her mouth, firmly but gently gripped by the neck or shoulders. Relocations like these may enable the female to hunt in different parts of her range, or they might be a strategy to avoid predators or parasites.

The cubs suckle for up to 12 weeks, but from about eight weeks they start taking solid food brought to them by their mother. The cubs are usually weaned by the age of three months and are able to move around with the mother, although somewhat ineptly at times. At this stage she usually leads them to her kills and they then feed themselves.

Although not nearly as social as lions, leopard mothers groom their cubs by licking and nibbling at their bodies, and by washing their faces. No doubt there are elements of family bonding as well as hygiene involved in grooming, and the cubs reciprocate by grooming one another as well as their mother.

In their play together, the cubs gradually learn to hunt, and to practise stalking and pouncing. Initial efforts at hunting and killing at about three to four months are seldom successful, but gradually the predatory skills are honed. Mothers sometimes assist in the learning process by bringing freshly killed prey to the youngsters. By worrying the carcass, pouncing on it, shaking it and dragging it about, the cubs learn to bite at the throat and to use their paws with claws extended to grasp and manoeuvre the prey. Sometimes the mother leopard may even bring live prey for the tutoring of her cubs. In this exploratory and learning phase of their lives leopard cubs are curious and mischievous, investigating anything that moves. If uncertain of what they are dealing with they approach cautiously, dabbing or swatting at animals such as leguaans, tortoises or even porcupines, from which they usually learn a sharp, unpleasant lesson.

From about four months of age cubs start killing small animals such as hares, mongooses, or rodents. By the age of six months they can stalk and catch fairly agile animals such as vervet monkeys and young antelope. By their first birthday, leopard cubs are almost adult-sized, and a month or two later they are able to hunt efficiently and feed themselves. The cubs may leave their mother at any time between 12 and 18 months of age, sometimes living independently, but within the maternal territory, or taking up a nomadic existence. Young females can come into oestrus for the first time at 21 months and are successfully mated at about two years of age.

The tolerance of a leopard mother for her cubs may extend into adulthood and there are records of female leopards and grown offspring affectionately greeting one another after long periods of separation – behaviour not recorded in cheetah. Despite their strong instincts as loners, therefore, there are several situations in which two leopards can be seen together, amicably resting on the same rock, whether a courting pair or a mother with a grown cub.

✳

As a leopard moves through its territory, following paths, checking on scratching trees, depositing scent, calling at its boundaries and listening for a neighbour's response, it is also alert to possible contact with prospective prey. When hungry, however, there is likely to be more purpose in the quest for something to eat. Hunting activity and the technique used to deliver a meal is highly variable and

The jumbled mass of granite boulders, typical of the Skukuza area of the Kruger National Park, forms many overhangs and caves which serve as nursery dens for leopard cubs.

depends on local conditions and the range of prey available. Hunting by a leopard follows the pattern of search, stalk, rush and kill. Sometimes, however, it is the seeming anticlimax of a chance meeting resulting in a kill.

Leopards detect suitable prey by sight, sound and smell. Interpretation of leopard tracks in the sandy Kalahari environment, as described by Koos Bothma and Elias le Riche, showed a leopard spotting a gemsbok cow and calf at a distance of more than two kilometres and then stalking them, using one of the typical long red sand dunes as cover. The leopard returned to the dune crest only once, apparently to have a look at the gemsbok and to judge their position. It then continued to stalk from behind the dune, only cresting again to charge the pair, killing the calf.

Leopards react to distress calls of prey animals. This fact is well known and often feared in the rainforest in parts of West and equatorial Africa, where hunters practise duiker calling as a decoy. The hunter takes up a position, usually among the plank buttresses of a tall forest tree, from where he has a good view of converging game trails. He then imitates the distress call of a duiker to attract a resident territorial male duiker to within range of his shotgun. This method works well, but can also result in the unwelcome sight of a leopard coming to investigate, as was once explained to me with graphic gestures by a Bété hunter in Côte d'Ivoire!

Leopards sometimes spot suitable prey at a distance and then start a very determined stalk. In the early stages the leopard moves quickly, at an intent trot, the head carried forward and the tail hanging low, not curled up as when patrolling. The approach is irregular, with movement arrested by the leopard freezing whenever the prey looks around alertly. The stalking leopard may freeze in a standing position, or slowly sink down onto its belly. When the prey resumes feeding or some other activity the leopard advances, using sloping ground, trees, bushes, long grass, termite mounds, rocks, or other natural feature as cover. The distance over which the stalk takes places varies – longer in more open territory and shorter in densely wooded habitats.

The stalk ends in a pounce onto the prey, or a charge if the intended victim has not sensed the approaching danger. Generally, larger prey animals

variations have been recorded, for example grey duikers which have been bitten behind the ears and into the cranium, and rodents which are either caught in the mouth and crushed, or swatted with the paws.

Leopards do not always attack helpless prey, and there are many records of them being on the receiving end of serious injuries from warthogs and baboons. Adult wildebeest, zebra, giraffe, sable antelope and gemsbok, and no doubt other species, too, will defend their young against predators and they are often successful in driving off a leopard. Porcupines are particularly capable of defending themselves by erecting their quills and slapping with their armed tails, in the process often impaling their attacker's paws or face. Any

Right: A leopard only unleashes its final charge when it is fairly close to its prey and the chances of success are high.
Opposite: Ever alert, an impala ram scans the bush, searching for any signs or sounds of danger.

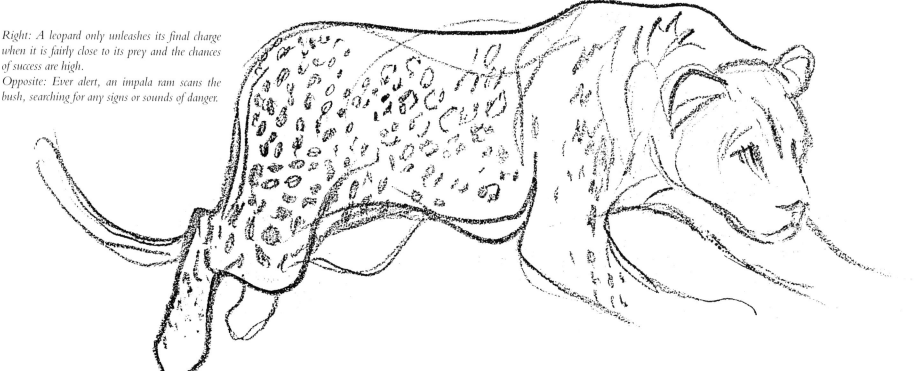

are detected and startled at greater distances than smaller animals. Usually the chase is short as the leopard, unlike the cheetah, is not built for speed and most of the leopard's larger prey animals can easily outrun it. Without the vital elements of surprise and confusion, the leopard stands little chance of making a kill. Only about one in ten leopard chases ends in success.

The leopard usually kills by a bite to the throat or nape of the neck, causing death by strangulation or severing of the spinal cord. With prey up to the size of impala, the leopard may suffocate the victim by clamping its jaws over the muzzle while holding the animal down. There are also records of a leopard breaking the neck of a bushbuck in an attack. With smaller animals other

leopard attempting to kill a porcupine stands a good chance of losing an eye, or suffering the agony of a quill embedded in its mouth.

If taken by night, baboons are considered fair game for a leopard, but it is a rash decision to take a member of a baboon troop during the day. Adult males will quickly rush to the victim's assistance and attack a leopard en masse, either putting it to flight or tearing it to pieces with their vicious, razor-sharp fangs.

After having made a kill, a leopard invariably moves its prey to cover. The cat clamps its powerful jaws onto the victim's neck straddling the body with its front legs and, by holding its head up and raising the neck and forequarters of the prey off the ground, it drags or carries it along. The prey is gutted at the

site of the kill, or somewhere en route to the shelter. Invariably this is done before the leopard tries to hoist its prey up a tree – thus substantially lightening the burden. The viscera are either left exposed or, occasionally, covered by leaves or litter being scraped over them.

When leopards kill birds, they use their teeth to pluck most of the feathers before feeding. Prey with long hair or fur, such as carnivores or young antelope, are also often partially 'plucked', especially at the point where the leopard starts feeding (which is usually on the prey's opened body cavity, chest, or rump).

✳

It is extremely difficult for observers to piece together the full range of a leopard's diet in a densely bushed environment where the animal cannot always be followed closely. This has resulted in most of the classic sources of information on the diet of the leopard and the other large cats being somewhat biased toward the kills of larger animals on which the leopards may feed for some time, and of which there are usually identifiable remains.

In many areas, such as rainforests and the macchia of the Cape mountains, identification of prey based on direct observation is impossible, and, until recently, the diet of leopards living in these environments remained a mystery. But now, with the technique of scat analysis – the identification of prey species

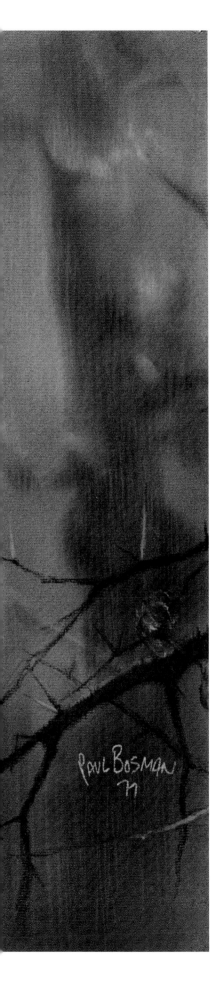

from the remains in the droppings of cats in the form of hair, teeth, hooves, claws, scales, feathers and small bones – it has become possible to expand our knowledge of the leopard's ecological niche to a far greater degree.

Unquestionably the leopard has a more varied diet than any of the other large cats. In Africa alone, it has been recorded taking well over 45 species of the larger mammals, as well as at least 30 species of rodents and other small mammals. Domestic pets, livestock and poultry are also taken, as well as wild birds, reptiles, fish, crabs, frogs, snails, beetles and occasionally other invertebrates. Leopards will scavenge if the opportunity presents itself – male leopards sometimes robbing their mates of their kills and even refusing to share with their own offspring. Leopards rob cheetah of their prey when they can, and feed off the carcasses of large animals such as African elephants, which they would not normally kill themselves. In short, a leopard will eat almost any animal it comes across, dead or alive – a key factor in its survival. For unusual leopard meals, however, few examples can compete with the well-documented record of a leopard taking a very young elephant calf up a tree in the Kruger National Park. Presumably it had killed the young pachyderm itself, as infant mortality from natural causes is very low in the park.

For a very long time there has been a widespread belief in Africa, referred to by Patrick Hamilton as 'part of the leopard's mythology', that baboons and bushpigs form the main prey of this cat. Many of the earlier writers on the

Opposite: Ever the watcher – in the African veld the leopard sees all, but is itself seldom seen.
Right: Whilst stalking prey – especially if cover is sparse – the leopard often freezes, remaining completely immobile, to avoid detection.

This page, and opposite: Adult male baboons act as sentinels for their troop, and will alert all to the presence of a leopard with loud barks and screams. If so detected the cat will saunter off, giving every impression of disdain for the primates.

to be incidental kills and then usually of young animals. The adults, potentially formidable adversaries, are seldom tackled.

Contrary to the belief that leopards always take their kills up a tree to cache them, this is a regular habit only where necessary to avoid losing the kill to lions, spotted hyaenas or jackals. Also, it is only possible to hoist a kill up a tree if there are suitable trees nearby. In a study undertaken in the Kalahari only six out of 38 kills observed were hoisted into trees – and on each occasion the hoisting was precipitated by the appearance of other predators. The other kills were either of a size that could be consumed in one sitting, or were dragged under the cover of a bush or tree and were consumed on the ground.

In another study, in the Matobo Hills in Zimbabwe, only one kill out of 37 was hoisted into a tree – and in this environment suitable trees are plentiful. Neither lions, hyaenas nor jackals are present in this area, however, so presumably the leopard had no need to expend the extra energy. Similar behaviour has been shown in parts of Namibia where there are no hyaenas and the leopards consume their prey on the ground. Conversely, in the Kruger National Park and the Serengeti, where lions and hyaenas are abundant, leopards invariably take their kill up trees. And even then, as recently witnessed at Mala Mala, lions will sometimes determinedly climb trees themselves to rob leopards of their dinner. Leopards do, however, simplify their task sometimes by first having a good feed on the ground and then hoisting the lighter remains of their kill up the tree.

In keeping with its solitary lifestyle the leopard has little patience with other predators or scavengers. Not only does it often chase competing species such as cheetah and black-backed jackal,

natural history of the continent referred to leopards being instrumental in keeping populations of baboons and bushpigs in check. It is certainly true that leopards kill baboons from time to time in areas as far apart as the Cape Mountains, the Matobos in Zimbabwe, and Kenya, but nowhere has the baboon been shown to be the major prey of the leopard. Bushpig and warthog are killed by leopard and there are many records of this, but again they seem

it kills them as well. Among the records are those of leopards killing cheetah and hanging them up in trees without feeding on them, and there is a report from Londolozi in South Africa of a leopard picking up an African wild dog that had been killed by lions, and hoisting it up a tree as well.

Leopards are well known as killers of dogs and jackals. Hans Kruuk and Myles Turner reported on a leopard in the Ngorongoro crater in Tanzania that had such a taste for jackals that it killed 11 in one month and only two Grant's gazelle. There are also many records of leopards eating their own kind killed in territorial battles or scavenged. A leopard skull in my collection – that of an old male – comes from a cat that was killed and partly devoured by another leopard quite close to Skukuza in the Kruger National Park.

✳

Situations of conflict between leopards and humans is as old as the tradition of keeping domestic animals in Africa, and applies equally to the other large predators – lion, cheetah, caracal, black-backed jackal and spotted hyaena. The essence of this antagonism lies in the fact that humans' livestock – poultry, sheep, goats and calves, as well as domestic pets – fall into the size class of the leopard's prey. Furthermore, these species, by comparison with similar-sized wild ungulates, are generally slower and far less able to escape or defend themselves against a leopard. They sleep in tightly packed, unalert groups, or are held in pens, and provide easy pickings for a cat with an opportunistic frame of mind.

Most pastoral people in Africa have evolved fairly efficient means of countering depredations on their livestock, and most tribes have traditional ways of hunting the large cats, whether with spears or poisoned arrows, whilst others have perfected various kinds of traps. Among some tribesmen, such as the Matabele of Zimbabwe, the killing of leopards was elevated to a test of manhood. The Matabele leopard-killing rite required the hunter to face the leopard armed only with a short, thorny branch of an acacia tree and a knobkierie – a short stick ending in a knob made from hardwood, and used as a club. The leopard would be tracked until it was brought to bay, whereupon the hunter then approached it, thorn branch in one hand and knobkierie in the other. The trick was to entice the leopard to spring at the man, who would use the thorny branch as a shield. This meant that the leopard would have to clear the branch to get at its assailant. If the cat succeeded, it would be dealt a killing blow to the head with the knobkierie. If the hunter's aim was off, he had only the thorny branch to ward off the leopard, and he could count on a serious mauling or death.

The arrival of firearms, and poisons such as strychnine, opened up new dimensions in leopard-killing proficiency. The growing numbers of people and livestock occupying

Opposite, and above: Leopards are still found in habitats as diverse as the rainforests of equatorial Africa and the semi-deserts of the south, such as the sun-baked rocks and hills of the Augrabies Falls National Park. Here the rock hyrax and springbok are the most abundant prey animals.

the land resulted in increasing conflict with wildlife, and increasing numbers of leopards being killed. The leopard as a species was consequently eliminated from large parts of its historical range. In the mountains of the Western Cape where Europeans first settled in 1652, and where the landscape has long since been tamed, the leopard survived comfortably until about 1910. Since then its range has declined dramatically and reasonable populations are now found only in the most remote areas where several hundred animals may still survive.

Records show that over the 24-year period from 1931 to 1955 a total of 947 leopards were declared to the authorities as having been killed legally. This indicated a heavy offtake from the population, as many more were probably killed illegally. From this average of 39 leopards killed each year, the current figure has dropped to about 28 leopards per year, but from an area less than half the size of that reflected in the earlier period. Present stock losses to leopards run at approximately 666 small and 24 large stock animals a year, or about 25 head of stock for each leopard legally killed.

Notwithstanding its persecution, the leopard has always held an honoured position in African society. In recent South African history President Nelson Mandela posthumously conferred the 'Order of the Leopard' on Helen Joseph, the revered anti-apartheid activist. Not only is wearing the skin of a leopard

*A leopard in the Shire Valley of Malawi takes a
yellow baboon aloft in a sycamore fig. Here it can
feed away from any disturbance.*

the prerogative of persons of rank, but the leopard also features prominently in folklore and witchcraft. In West Africa there are, or were, numerous secret societies which chose the leopard as their totem. Some of these societies indulged in ritual murder in which the victim was clawed and scratched with artificial leopard claws made from iron. This left no doubt in the minds of the victim's fellows that the execution had been carried out by the Leopard Men.

There is also a continent-wide belief in the power of leopard whiskers to cause death. The whiskers are cut up into small pieces and fed to a victim in his food or drink with the purpose of killing him. Leopard skins with their whiskers cut off have been the bane of safari hunters in many areas of Africa. Even scientific specimens are not immune, and Rosevear mentions that of 25 West African leopard skins in the British Museum, only one has its full complement of whiskers. In 22 cases the whiskers have all been cut off. I once examined five leopard skins in a government store in Malawi – and sure enough found that most of the whiskers were missing.

The mystique of the leopard has also been strong in the West, and although the leopard does not feature as prominently as the lion in heraldry, the tradition of leopard skin aprons for regimental bandsmen is widespread, especially in the British Army.

✻

Translocation, as a well-meant alternative to killing stock-raiding leopards, has been attempted over the past three decades. The justification for capturing problem animals and then releasing them alive in some distant national park was guided by the mistaken belief that the leopard was an endangered species. Translocation was justified on the grounds – highly fashionable in the West – that it was better to 'save' an animal that was killing livestock than to destroy it. Although the policy was pursued in Zimbabwe, Namibia and South Africa, it was only in Kenya that it was carried out on a significant scale – with more than 200 translocations taking place. Some successes were achieved and some leopards that were settled in new areas supplemented the local population well. From the limited data available and from a study by Patrick Hamilton of 15 leopards translocated over a three-year period, however, the overall conclusion can only be that the policy was a misguided and costly failure.

Most of the translocated leopards remained in the vicinity of the release site for only a few days before moving off for long distances. Some of them showed very strong homing instincts indeed and started moving steadily in the direction of their original home ranges. Here they usually resumed their stock-killing habits and were either killed or re-trapped. One leopard from near Gilgil in Kenya was trapped and moved to the Nairobi National Park to be released. Fourteen months later it was trapped 140 kilometres away from the release point and in the same general area from where it had originally been removed. Other leopards also managed to return to their original home ranges – some were trapped or killed along the way, and only a few ever remained in the areas to which they were moved.

In the case of most translocated leopards, their subsequent movements extended over areas of 100 to 600 square kilometres – more than adequate to take them far beyond the boundaries of all but the largest protected areas.

The homing ability of leopards has been adequately demonstrated on many occasions. One animal with this ability was known to Hamilton as 'Leopard 97'. The story of this animal also demonstrated the futility of trans-locating stock killers as a management policy. 'Leopard 97' was originally trapped as a stock raider on a farm near Naivasha and moved to Lake Nakuru National Park some 50 kilometres distant. He soon returned home, however, and was trapped whilst killing more livestock. This time he was moved 140 kilometres to the southwest, but once more returned and was caught on the same farm – this being the third time he was captured. 'Leopard 97' was then moved 110 kilometres away to the forests on the slopes of Mount Kenya and released. A year later he was again trapped killing livestock nearby and moved 130 kilometres to Meru. Within two months he was trapped for the fifth time, after again killing livestock, and moved to the Tana River.

The Kalahari recently presented a similar saga. This concerned an adult female leopard trapped on a farm in Namibia, in an area adjoining the Kalahari Gemsbok National Park. The leopard was moved some 50 kilometres into the park and released. Within days she was back on the farm killing livestock. Captured a second time, she was moved 80 kilometres eastward and released in the Nossob riverbed. Again she homed within a few days, killed livestock and had to be caught for a third time.

In the mountains of the Cape a stock-raiding leopard was trapped and translocated, but it moved back a distance of 60 kilometres to its original home where it again caught stock.

The studies of 'Leopard 97' and the Cape and Kalahari leopards indicate not only the homing ability of these animals, but also seem to show that once a leopard has tasted easy pickings, it is inclined to continue taking domestic stock. There have been many other examples of leopard translocations ending in failure. The most dangerous cases concerned man-eating leopards trapped and translocated in Kenya which, after release in the Tsavo National Park, determinedly went after humans. Had the leopards succeeded in killing more people, the consequences could have been disastrous for the wildlife authorities and their relations with the park's neighbours.

One of the motivations for translocating stock-raiding leopards was to supplement ostensibly depleted leopard populations in wildlife areas. It is clear from our understanding of the leopard's social organization, however, that any translocation into an occupied area has the cards heavily stacked against success. The intrusion of strangers is seldom tolerated. Even fighting between neighbours who know one another is sometimes so fierce that it results in serious injury or death. Studies on other carnivores indicate that conflicts with total strangers are far more serious than clashes with a known 'dear-enemy' or 'rival-friend'. Thus it is likely that introduced leopards facing an unknown territory holder in a strange environment, possibly also to some extent hampered by the trauma of capture and translocation, may be at a serious disadvantage. These weaknesses may also serve to embolden the territory holder's attack. In part this could explain why introduced animals move so fast and so far.

Clearly the conservation objective is not served if the translocated animal is killed by a resident animal, or if the resident is displaced by the introduced animal. Even if there is no physical contact between an introduced animal and a resident, it is likely that the stranger will keep moving when confronted by the territorial marking sites and scent of the territory holder. While translocated

The plains zebra is widely distributed across East and southern Africa in savanna and woodland habitats. Foals are occasionally taken by leopards.

female leopards may be accepted by resident males, they are unlikely to be tolerated by resident females. Therefore, unless there is a vacant territory, there is little chance of a leopard translocation achieving the objective of allowing the stranger to become integrated into the local leopard land-tenure system, and of it breeding with the locals.

There is evidence from studies of mountain lions in North America, which have a social system similar to the leopard, that territories vacated through the death of a resident can be filled only by a new animal of the same sex. For a translocation to succeed, therefore, it requires not only a vacant territory, but a territory suiting the sex of the translocated animal.

Sometimes biology is perverse when dealing with humankind's more esoteric objectives such as shuffling animals around the globe. There is evidence that translocated animals may not settle easily in an area, even if there are no signs at all of resident animals. Again, the evidence comes from studying the mountain lion, and it indicates that a transient or wandering animal is unlikely to develop an attachment to an area from which the species has been eliminated. The logic is clear when seen in context, as the purpose of the territorial system is to share resources among a population in a way which promotes the species' welfare rather than the individual's. The purpose of a male leopard's territory is not only to provide him with food and living space, but also to provide mating opportunities. If a newly-arrived male animal in a vacant area has no chance of contacting a female, then that territory is obviously not biologically viable and he will move on in search of a more suitable one.

Generally, wandering animals can move through and out of any but a few of the largest African national parks in the space of a few days. Once outside the park they are again at risk, and nothing will have been achieved by the translocation.

There are other biological aspects which would warrant consideration in any assessment of proposed leopard translocation. In the first instance there is the matter of genetics. Within Kenya the highland leopards are larger and darker than the smaller and paler leopards of Tsavo. Moving animals from one gene pool to the other may, therefore, be an unwarranted interference for genetic reasons alone. On balance, therefore, it is a far more sensible policy to shoot stock-raiding leopards rather than to translocate them.

In recent decades the commercial trade in leopard skins has become an added spur to hunting the species – both legally (usually leopards that are killing livestock) and illegally. By 1969 an estimate of the number of leopards killed to support the fur trade was as high as 50 000 animals a year. This estimate was derived from about 20 000 skins reaching the markets in North America and Europe. Furthermore, allowance was made for trapped or wounded leopards lost in the field, for damaged skins being rejected from the trade, and for the death of orphaned cubs. These circumstances would most likely have accounted for more leopards than those whose skins were successfully exported from Africa. The estimate of these additional leopard mortalities was put at 30 000 animals, but there is no way of determining whether this estimate was anywhere near the truth.

The concerted and sustained efforts of the conservation lobby in the West have now stopped the trade in leopard skins. Although it is not disputed that the trade in leopard skins was excessive, and that it was impacting seriously on many leopard populations, it is equally clear that for the leopard the killing of the trade was a victory in which the winner's losses were as great as those of the losers. In many areas the leopard skin trade was sustained by the pelts obtained from livestock killers that were shot. The livestock owners derived compensation for lost animals from the leopard skins traded. An uneasy cohabitation of human and leopard was possible while the leopard was paying for his keep in this way. Once that avenue was shut off, however, the livestock owners had no more hope of compensation and therefore had a major incentive simply to kill off the remaining leopards. Thus, it is likely that the conservationists have been responsible for more leopard killing and the total elimination of leopards from more areas than were the hunters.

The opportunity that existed for the development of a rational, sustained harvesting system – one that would have allowed leopards and pastoralists to live together *and* to keep a viable fur trade going – was squandered. Subsequent events of great ecological significance, such as the extended droughts of the 1970s and 1980s, had further heavy impacts on the African environment, including overgrazing by domestic stock, the loss of wildlife and ultimately the loss of even more leopard range. Despite all of this, recent estimates put the number of leopards in Africa at somewhere between 200 000 and 700 000 – this being nowhere near the extinction level that ardent Western conservationists have claimed for so long.

The only really honest argument against the harvesting of African leopard skins is the possibility that an open market may conceivably represent a threat to leopards in Asia – where they *are* threatened. One such subspecies is the Amur leopard *Panthera pardus orientalis* which inhabits the border areas of north-eastern China and the Russian Far East along the Amur River, and whose numbers in the wild are now estimated at only about 40 individuals.

Future prospects for the leopard over vast parts of Africa's rangelands, woodlands and savannas where humans and livestock are increasing are not particularly good. The leopard has demonstrated itself the most adaptable of the large carnivores, however, and it survives in many areas where lion, cheetah and hyaena have long since been eliminated. The leopard as a species, however, is not in any present danger of extinction.

The gradual decline in leopard numbers and range in some countries has resulted in the development of various local conservation strategies for leopards. In the case of the Western Cape of South Africa, a strategy similar to that of Operation Tiger in India has been proposed. This will depend upon the cooperation of government and private landowners to create sanctuaries linking various isolated sub-populations of leopards by means of corridors where they will be tolerated, and farmers compensated for stock losses. In these corridor areas there will be hunting of stock raiders to ensure that the leopard population density stays below the threshold where livestock owners

Being anything but timid, the sable antelope will defend itself aggressively against all large predators.

will want them totally exterminated. This should ensure that a sufficient number of non-territorial animals will survive to disperse through these areas from one high-density sanctuary or core area to another.

Management of the core areas will be directed at maintaining optimum leopard habitat by carrying optimum populations of leopard prey. In this way it is planned to maintain a genetically viable population of leopards in the long term.

The leopard, as one of the big five game trophies of Africa, has always had a value to the trophy-hunting industry. In the past, most safari hunting took place in East Africa where game was abundant. The growth of human and live-stock populations, with the consequent decline in game numbers as well as a number of ill-conceived restrictions on hunting has, however, virtually killed off the industry over most of sub-Saharan Africa. With the decline in the north, the emphasis of the industry has shifted to the southern African countries.

In these arid southern savannas, the hunting industry has evolved into a paying partner of the cattle industry. One of the prizes remains the leopard, Africa's ultimate spotted cat, and a trophy leopard will add up to US$ 4 000 on top of daily rates. This ends up giving the leopard a significant cash value. There is a considerable incentive, therefore, to maintain breeding populations of leopards to service the hunting industry. The extermination of leopards as a result of trophy-hunting is most unlikely.

THE LION

Left: To many people the full-blooded roar of a lion in the wild represents the essence of Africa. Right: The regal bearing of a lion is enhanced by the glory of his mane which, in biological terms, increases his size, making him more intimidating.

To follow a pair of maned lions – brothers in their prime – as they regally patrol the borders of their territory is a truly unforgettable experience. Paul and I were privileged to share this adventure in the Kruger National Park one moonlit night. Although all cats select ways of proclaiming and marking the boundaries of their territories from the same basic set of techniques, none do it on quite the same grand scale as the lion.

We knew that the two males in question occupied a territory of about 200 square kilometres in the Nwaswitshaka Valley. Here the terrain consists of gently undulating bush country, cut by many dry, sandy riverbeds with thicketed banks. Isolated piles of huge, jumbled, granite boulders form small hills – one of the most prominent of which is the solid dome of Thekwane, so named in the language of the Tsonga people.

The group of lions that lived in the area were known as the Thekwane pride. It comprised the two dark-maned adult males and four lionesses with cubs of different ages. Often the pride would climb to the top of the hills where they would spend some time resting during the day. Presumably they

enjoyed the benefits of whatever breeze there was to take the edge off the often oppressive heat of the Lowveld summer. Perhaps the hills also offered a vantage point from where they could keep watch for potential prey or intruders.

On this memorable night the lionesses and their eight cubs were lying on Thekwane's bald summit, while the two males had moved off to devote themselves to the more serious business of border patrol. The two were about 300 metres apart and about half a kilometre from Thekwane when one of them, facing east to where he presumably imagined his opposition to be, began a magnificent series of roars.

At first he gave a few low, long calls. (These vocalizations are better described as hoots or hums, rather than grunts which are sharper, guttural, explosive sounds. Growls are rattling and heavy, while roars are full, resonant, echoing challenges.) We supposed that the lion's calls were to tell the rest of the pride where he was, for they immediately pricked up their ears and stared intently in his direction. The second male, from his post, answered the first with the same low hoot and we now knew that the stage had been set.

This page, and opposite: Seemingly lazy, lions spend most of their day resting. They are ever watchful, though, and whilst guinea fowl may be mere distractions, the approach of impala can transform a lioness into immediate action.

Following the sounds we soon caught sight of the first male. He was the very epitome of power and majesty as he stood, head held high, ears cocked, gazing intently into the gathering darkness to the east. Then he began to roar – loudly and in earnest – the tremendous sounds starting deep inside his body. With the lion's head straining forward, mouth open and lips extended like a trumpet, the roars burst forth. The great chest heaved, the contraction beginning at the lion's hips with his belly pressing up against his innards. The rolling, thunderous sound reverberated through the trees and the dense thickets.

The performance consisted of eight full roars, followed by a series of 14 grunts, steadily diminishing in volume, and with more time between each utterance. The great roaring machine was slowly winding down. As the last grunt faded, the lion sank to the ground, where he lay, head up and still facing the east, seemingly relieved of a great burden. The bush was silent, Nature stilled by the bellowing.

A few moments later, while Paul and I were still recovering from the numbing experience of being only a few paces away, the companion lion burst out with his own impressive contribution. It was equal in power to that of the first male, and our ears rang once more. There were fewer grunts at the end, however, and the return to the silence of the night seemed more abrupt.

After a while the second lion appeared, his features slowly taking shape as he seemed to float toward our vehicle out of the gloom. He sniffed intently at a nearby bush and then flopped down. The first male, as though it was again his turn to perform, stood up again and started walking along the track. He sniffed at the same dark, green-leaved *Euclea* bush and rubbed his cheeks against its branches and foliage, his nose held high. Then he turned his back to it, lifted his tail in a graceful arc and squirted several jets of urine at the bush, while simultaneously raking the ground with his hind paws and scattering dead leaves, grass and other litter. After about five scrapes with each hind paw he moved off at a steady, relaxed and confident pace. Behind him, next to and on the bush, was the unambiguous message for all other lions to see and smell. He was master of this land.

The second male rose slowly, then stretched like a kitten, his chest almost touching the ground as he pulled down on his shoulder muscles, tail flicking the air with imperious strokes, hind legs tensed and pushing firmly against the ground. His mouth opened in a yawn, exposing huge white canines and a pink tongue. He then recomposed himself and followed his companion, sniffing at the anointed bush in passing.

With the two of us following as best we could, the Thekwane pair continued with their patrol. After some time, from far to the east, their roars were answered. This seemed to reassure them that all was well – their neighbour had acknowledged their presence and they could now rejoin their pride and turn their attention to hunting. Or rather, they could return to following the hunting lionesses, so that they could take their fill from whatever kill the females made.

Lions patrol their territories regularly and thoroughly, sometimes doing nothing else all night long. They do not roar regularly, but may sound off at intervals throughout the night. They are more likely to roar just after sunset and, particularly, in the early hours just before dawn. A full-blooded roar can be heard by humans at a range of up to eight kilometres on a still night, but lions can probably hear the sound over an even greater distance. They answer the challenges of their neighbours in like vein and sometimes, as is evident from listening to the changing position of two groups of roaring lions, adjacent prides will move closer toward their mutual boundaries.

This vocal thrust and parry of neighbouring prides is a mechanism for reinforcing pride boundaries, minimizing combat, identifying territory holders and for communicating with other lions moving into or through the vicinity. The prides may meet up and fight, but it is more likely that they will move closer and then withdraw. If they are established neighbours, and they respect each other's turf, there is no need to fight. Talk is cheaper than war in terms of the amount of energy expended and the risk of injury.

✳

The lion is the only permanently social, or group-living cat. All other cats are solitary, adults consorting only briefly to breed and mothers alone caring for their offspring until they can fend for themselves. Cheetahs can be something of an exception, with groups comprising a mother and her grown cubs, or adult siblings who have remained together.

Just as the elephant's basic social unit consists of the matriarch and her immediate family, so are the lioness and her offspring the focus of lion society, the pride. Sometimes the lionesses of the pride are sisters, but the average degree of female relatedness is usually that of full cousins. There are also claims of unrelated lionesses, supposedly nomadic and usually immature strangers, being allowed to join an established pride. But evidence of this is flimsy, and more commonly any strangers are swiftly seen off.

Female cubs born to pride lionesses usually remain bonded for life to the group, but males do not figure as permanent members. Male cubs are ousted at puberty, while the two adult males that usually accompany a pride occupy their positions by right of conquest. Although these breeding coalitions may sometimes be between brothers or cousins, recent findings indicate that it is more common for non-relatives to become allies in taking over a pride. Their reign is generally short-lived, however, and it is a few years at the most before they are, in turn, routed by younger, stronger males. Noisy and fierce though these battles of succession may be, serious injuries are rare. The vanquished males often become nomads, wandering over large distances, eventually settling in an area not claimed by other lions. Occasionally, defending males are fatally wounded in the fray, or suffer disabling injuries leading inevitably to a lingering death.

The presence of adult males is not always a prerequisite in pride structure, for groups consisting only of females and their young have been seen in the Mala Mala Game Reserve in South Africa, Nairobi National Park in Kenya, and the Savuti Marsh area of Botswana. Why this pride structure occurs is not clearly understood, but there are some interesting observations.

In Savuti, biologist Petri Viljoen noted two female prides which shared a group of three males. He concluded that birth synchronization by the females, which effectively limited mating chances for the males, may have played a role. It is possible, however, that the reasons for the disappearance of pride males could simply lie in their being overtaken by wanderlust of some leonine kind.

All three of the above-mentioned areas have a common characteristic, and herein may lie a clue to the pride structure observed there. Mala Mala, Savuti and Nairobi all have an abundance of prey animals relative to the number of lions. And so, where there is such a ready larder and the males can get plenty to eat (even if it means having to make their own kills), such a loosely structured pride system could suit them very well. For instance, if they mated with lionesses in several female-only prides, they would then effectively be 'owners' of a much larger territory than could be held by a single pride.

Another shared characteristic is that in all three areas there appears to be a much lower adult male to female sex ratio than in areas where the conventional pride structure holds sway. If there were more adult males in the above-mentioned three areas, then access to females for each individual male would be limited simply by the presence of other competing males. There is no indication that fewer male cubs are born in these areas, however. Certainly mortality is higher among male cubs than females, but this is consistently the case in all lion populations because male cubs are more adventurous and may stray, get lost or be left behind. Furthermore, if this (that is the birth of fewer male cubs) was a valid explanation, then surely one could expect a more widespread occurrence of female-only prides? This is not so. At Mala Mala, up until 1993, only a game fence – no barrier for lions – separated it from the Kruger National Park, where the social structure is more conventional.

One plausible explanation for the paucity of adult males in these areas lies in the fact that Mala Mala and Savuti adjoin safari-hunting areas where male lions are highly sought after as trophies. Furthermore, Mala Mala and Nairobi are also bordered by cattle-ranching and settled areas where nomadic or wandering male lions are shot on sight.

Whatever the reason for or combination of factors giving rise to female-only prides may be, the available information is too sketchy to allow a firm conclusion. The female-only pride structure remains something of an enigma.

✳

The mating of lions is a grand affair. A lioness in oestrus is closely followed by the males of the pride. When she is ready to mate she indicates this by making advances to the male of her choice: typically, she walks in front of him, tail swept up high, inviting his attention. The male responds with dignity – at first just moving closer and lying down next to the receptive female. She may then playfully roll onto her side next to her chosen mate, swatting at his face with an extended paw and snarling at him. Then, snarling in response, he advances, his intention clear. In a final gesture of acceptance the female may roll over into a crouch as she is mounted.

Copulation is quick and noisy – lasting only a few seconds – being accompanied by much growling and whining on both parts. Towards the end, as an integral part of the ritual, the male tightly grips the nape of the lioness's neck. She will usually respond to the 'love bite' by twisting away, jumping up and, snarling viciously, slashing out at her mate's face with an open paw. But the apparent aggression soon dissipates, with the mating couple settling down relaxedly side by side, and with every indication of contentment.

After some 10 to 20 minutes, mating is repeated with the same choreographed steps. The routine can continue unabated, day and night, for several

Paul Bosman

Previous page: Throughout the course of mating, which lasts for up to two days, the lion never lets the lioness out of his sight.

Above: Wide-eyed, innocent and curious – a lion cub takes a keen interest in its surroundings, especially in anything that moves.

Opposite: Tiny, blind and helpless, newborn cubs are gently cared for by their mother.

days. The mating pair do not take any deliberate steps to avoid the other members of the pride and copulation often occurs in the presence of other lions. The pair are reluctant to go off hunting with the pride, however, and are often left behind while the others set off to find a meal.

A single male generally remains the consort of an oestrous lioness throughout the course of her receptive mating period, although some lionesses may mate with more than one male. This may happen if the male consort loses interest in the lioness, for example, presumably at the waning of her oestrous period. On the other hand, the lioness may abandon her partner to entice another. Such promiscuous female behaviour sometimes provokes brief fighting between the males in the pride, but generally males respect the rights of a companion who is mating with a lioness, and move off if threatened by her guardian.

Biologists have offered several explanations as to what benefits may result from a lioness copulating with more than one male. It is known that only approximately a third of all mating sessions result in pregnancy. So, if the chances of fertilization from a single mating are low and, as one report states, if fertilization occurs only on the fourth day of oestrus, it suggests that there is a high likelihood that multiple matings by a lioness may result in a litter where the cubs could have different fathers.

It may well be that the increased genetic diversity of her offspring is advantageous – perhaps the competition between the sperm of different males ensures that only the best sperm cells fertilize the ova. It could also be that males in a social system such as a pride may be more tolerant of cubs if they are instinctively uncertain of the parentage. Furthermore, the sharing of mating presumably guards against the formation of a strong pair bond, which could interfere with the collective devotion of all to the pride.

The most plausible explanation of multiple mating, however, is that the pride females may be attempting to increase the extent of their offspring's relatedness. If a pride's cubs are more closely related to one another, it fosters kin selection. The social and cooperative behaviour of lions, which benefits all members of a pride (such as hunting, communal suckling of young, mutual grooming and the banding together of young males from the same pride to take over another pride), all have more significance if there is a possibility that the cubs born of different mothers are closely related to one another.

After a gestation period of about 110 days the lioness finds a secluded spot away from the pride to give birth. Usually her litter will comprise one to four cubs – the average is three – but in rare instances five or six cubs are born. The cubs are tiny at birth, weighing no more than 1.5 kilograms, only one per cent of their adult size and weight. Blind and scarcely able to crawl, the newborn cubs are helpless. Their fluffy coats are heavily marked by dark rosettes – a phenomenon which can theoretically be traced back to some primaeval leopard-like ancestor.

Initially the cubs spend most of the time sleeping, well hidden in the den where their mother leaves them to hunt with the pride. But she returns regularly to suckle her offspring and may spend a great deal of time resting with them or near their hideout. The mother does not always enter the lair to feed her cubs. Instead she may approach closely and then call them, using a short, deep, humming sound. The cubs respond immediately, moving out

eagerly to latch onto their mother's conspicuous, swollen teats.

These early days of life are fraught with danger as, during the lioness's frequent absences from the den, the cubs are vulnerable to attack from hyaenas, leopards and black-backed jackals, all of which have been observed killing lion cubs. Buffalo and elephant have been known to trample them to death and there are even records of small cubs being killed by safari ants.

The cubs are kept hidden for six to eight weeks – not even other members of the pride see them during this time. At about two months, the cubs weigh roughly four kilograms and usually have their full complement of teeth, including molars. Now the cubs are ready for the next step of their lives – the all-important introduction to the pride. If the lair is far from where the pride is resting, the mother may have to help her offspring make the journey. She can easily carry the cubs in her mouth, but only one at a time. Once she gets them all to the pride, she introduces each of them into the circle – appearing very tense and wary whilst doing so.

Paul has been privileged to observe one such crucial event in Zimbabwe. The lioness was extremely cautious, slowly approaching the large pride male with a cub in her mouth. He, in turn, lay imperious, staring at the small fluffy thing. The mother gently placed the cub in front of him and stood back anxiously, watching him intently. After sniffing at the cub, he gently rubbed his chin on its back. Apparently satisfied, he then rolled over and let his great head flop to the ground as he stretched out to rest. The lioness then carefully

retrieved the cub and carried it to the other members of the pride, where it was sniffed at and carefully inspected by all.

Small cubs cannot keep up with the pride on long walks, so they may again be hidden while the pride hunts. After a kill has been made, the lioness then calls or fetches them. This usually occurs only after most of the kill has been consumed, and feeding is no longer the frenzied affair of the first few moments, when a small cub getting in a hungry lion's way is likely to be snapped at or cuffed.

Generally the lioness keeps her young cubs away from the potentially dangerous pride males and she also acts protectively towards her cubs in the presence of strange females. A lioness's control over her cubs is based on her short humming call to which the cubs respond by running to her. The lioness, however, is not in the same league as her elephant counterpart when it comes to mothering skills, as lion cubs can and do get lost or stray from the pride. There are also many records of cubs that have been found seemingly abandoned.

From about six months of age the male cubs grow faster than females, and

by nine or ten months the first signs of a ruff, later to become the mane, appear. The behaviour of male cubs by about one year of age is already consistent with that of their adult counterparts. For example, the young males hold back when the pride moves, rest a little way from the other members of the pride, and spend more time in grooming themselves and their developing manes. After the age of one year the cubs take more interest in the hunt, gradually learning to master hunting and killing techniques. By the time they are two years old the males are ready for independence. By that time their mother may be busy nursing her next litter, as females usually resume sexual activity when their cubs reach the age of about 18 months.

Cubs are allowed to suckle from other lionesses in the pride besides their mother. Some females are more tolerant of this than others, with the result that cubs suckle from them more frequently. Although this pattern usually benefits the cubs, it may sometimes lead to increased mortality of smaller cubs, who find themselves competing with another lioness's larger cubs for milk from their own mother. This behaviour may be particularly important during times of food scarcity when lionesses have less milk, for although the development of the pride's smallest cubs may be prejudiced as a result, it probably helps to ensure survival of the larger, stronger cubs whose own mothers' milk alone might not be enough. This altruistic behaviour may also enhance the prospects of cubs whose own mother may have been killed or seriously injured.

Another benefit of lionesses allowing the pride's other cubs to suckle from them is that it may effectively extend the period during which cubs receive milk as part of their diet. This may happen, for example, when the cubs of a lioness at the end of lactation are allowed to suckle with the younger cubs of another lioness in a much earlier stage of lactation.

Cubs generally suckle until they are about a year old, sometimes for a little longer. Although cubs may suckle at any time the mother allows it, most suckling occurs in the morning when the pride settles down to rest after the business of the night. Another period of intense suckling occurs during the late afternoon before the pride becomes active once again. While the cubs are too

Cubs grow rapidly if they get enough food, but their growth may be stunted if food is scarce. Weak cubs are vulnerable to disease, and fare poorly in competition with older cubs and adults for food. Some cubs starve; others are killed by adults. It is not unusual for half of any given litter to die during the first year – in fact, as many as 80 per cent of lion cubs do not survive beyond this point. Almost one third of all cub deaths are violent. Synchronously born cubs are more likely to survive than cubs born at greater intervals, because when several females are caring for cubs of the same age the pride's routine is more likely to be regulated to suit the youngsters.

Grooming, in addition to suckling, plays a highly significant part in strengthening the bond between a mother and her cubs. As the cubs mature, they respond to their mother's affection by grooming her, as well as their litter mates. As grooming involves licking or nuzzling one another, it is a strong contact-enhancing behaviour which strengthens social bonds and builds amicable relations within the pride. This may begin on the cub's part as a simple rubbing of its head or muzzle against its mother or a sibling, gradually developing into licking and more generalized rubbing between litter mates and their mother as they grow older. Grooming, apart from being a social activity, also has the practical hygienic advantage of allowing the animals to be cleaned by their companions. Grooming is especially noticeable and intense after the pride has been feeding, when many of the lions are somewhat blood-spattered and really do need a good cleaning off.

Play is an important aspect of a cub's life, whether it is play among litter mates, or a cub's more restrained play with an adult or older cubs. Among lions the major elements of play involve variations of stalking, chasing, catching and overpowering – all of these being basic ingredients of hunting and prey-manipulating behaviour.

Just like domestic kittens, lion cubs are attracted by movement. The gently flicking tail tip of an alert adult is sure to invite a bumbling attack from a cub, who will swat at it with its forepaws and then try to catch and bite it. Cubs frequently chase one another, rolling and tumbling about, and the art of the ambush is learnt early on. Fun-filled attacks on siblings are often launched from the cover of a resting adult, a fallen tree, a low bush, or any other place of concealment that presents itself.

Although the play behaviour of cubs prepares them for hunting, they seldom enact the most common killing manoeuvres such as the merciless stranglehold on the throat, or clamp on the muzzle. They do, however, practise

Above: A lioness moves her cubs by carrying them in her mouth if they are still too small to walk. Opposite: Play is an important element in the development of a cub as the youngster learns how to interact socially with other members of the pride, and to hunt – by stalking, chasing and catching.

small to move with the adult pride, they usually spend the entire night without their mother and thus without suckling. If the hunt has taken the lioness far away during the night, she may not even be able to return to her cubs for periods of 24 hours or more. There are records of lionesses being away from their cubs for as long as 36 hours at a time. As the lion's milk is rich, however, well-fed cubs can survive long periods without suckling quite comfortably.

The cessation of the lioness's lactation and, consequently, the weaning of her cubs, is a gradual process. It extends from the sixth or eighth month to the twelfth month. During the last few months of lactation the cubs suckle less, becoming more dependent on meat. They eat the flesh and organs of kills, chew on carcass scraps and bones, and generally become fully carnivorous.

The lioness may begin to experience some discomfort during suckling after about six months. She becomes less tolerant of her cubs' efforts to drink, and behaves more aggressively, snarling at the cubs and moving away repeatedly when they attempt to suckle. She may resort to lying on her belly to prevent the cubs from reaching her teats. Cubs object to this denial by whining and becoming even more persistent in their efforts to suckle. Gradually, however, a pattern of less frequent suckling sets in and the cubs are weaned.

The African wild dog is widespread across the savannas and plains and has little influence on the other large predators, mostly avoiding them.

the killing bite to the back of the neck, which is commonly used by cats when fighting rivals. As the cubs grow older their play becomes less exuberant and more oriented toward disciplined hunting behaviour.

If cubs are present during a period when a pride male is ousted, their lives are at risk. The strong new pride male may kill and even eat the small cubs of his predecessor. Thereby he ensures the early return to oestrus of their mother, and a mating opportunity for himself. By killing his predecessor's cubs he improves his own chances of having progeny, eliminates future competition his own cubs may have, and ensures that the lionesses spend their time protecting *his* genetic investment and not that of another male.

Subadult lions leaving their natal prides usually adopt a nomadic existence, moving around seemingly at random. There are, however, several restraints on their movements: they need to find food, so they tend to follow game; and they need to avoid settled prides who often attack nomads, driving them out of their territory and sometimes injuring them in the process.

Nomad groups may consist of lions of both sexes, and individuals are often members of the same litter, or different litters from the same pride. Occasionally they pick up strangers in the course of their wanderings and form a new pride. Breeding may occur among nomads, but the cubs seldom survive the critical first weeks when a nursing mother leaves her cubs hidden and depends on her pride mates to help keep her fed. The wanderings of present-day nomadic lions are confined to protected areas. Only in the Kalahari Desert in Botswana, the Kaokoveld in northwestern Namibia and less densely settled parts of the woodlands of Central Africa, do nomadic lions still have space enough to move.

If they are lucky they end up in a protected area – most, however, are killed.

In late 1987 the wanderings of a nomadic lion were recorded in Namibia. Researchers were able to piece together the movements – over a period of two months – of a five-year-old male with a distinctive spoor caused by an injury. The lion covered a distance of about 500 kilometres between the Ugab and Kuiseb rivers in the central Namib Desert. Along the way he killed two cows and a donkey, and his adventure only ended when he was captured by game rangers and moved to the Skeleton Coast Park, where he was fitted with a radio-transmitter collar before being released.

✳

Like other cats, lions adapt well to the particular circumstances in which they find themselves. They select their prey from the spectrum of available animals, but, given a choice, usually exhibit a definite preference for large ungulates. It has been argued that the social structure of lions has evolved from the necessity of cooperation in bringing down such large animals successfully.

Most studies have shown that lions' prey falls in the weight range of 20 to 800 kilograms in mass. This wide spectrum effectively includes warthog and gazelle at the lower end of the scale, and animals such as giraffe and Cape buffalo at the upper end. Occasionally lions in groups may attack and kill even heavier animals such as black rhinoceros, white rhinoceros and hippopotamus, but this is not the norm. Lions also take small animals, such as springhares and steenbok, and records show that Kalahari and Kruger lions regularly kill porcupines. This kind of prey animal is too small to contribute a major part to a lion's food intake, though, and it is unlikely that a pride would thrive and raise cubs on such meagre fare. Such small animals may, however, be used to tide lions over during hard times, especially in areas where larger game migrate and are therefore not always readily available.

The role of lions in a savanna ecosystem has long been a point of debate when planning wildlife management strategies for national parks in Africa. Early in the twentieth century many of these parks followed a blanket anti-predator policy. This meant that rangers shot lions and other predators on sight, believing that ungulates would then stand a better chance of survival.

In the years between 1902 and 1946, during the reign of the pioneering warden Lt Col Stevenson-Hamilton, thousands of lions were shot in South Africa's Kruger National Park. At the time it was assumed that lions and other predators were the main mechanism of population regulation acting upon

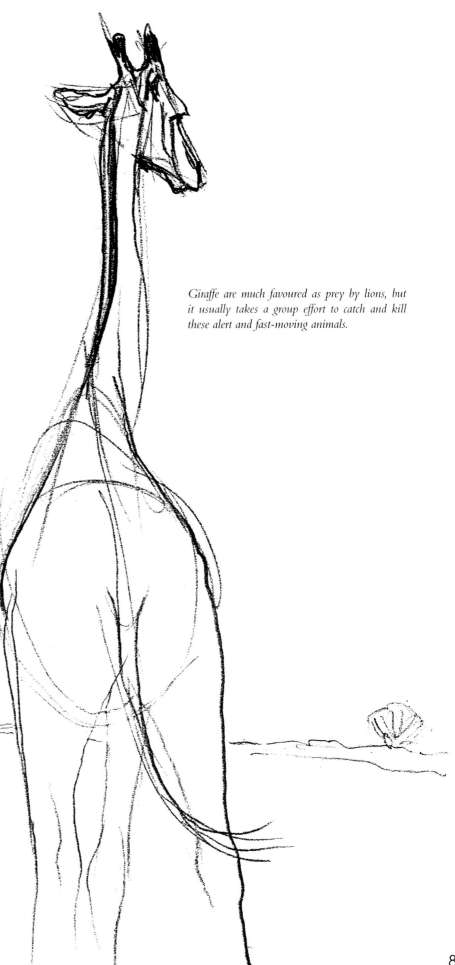

Giraffe are much favoured as prey by lions, but it usually takes a group effort to catch and kill these alert and fast-moving animals.

receive their meat sprinkled with various vitamin and mineral supplements.

In times gone by, many nature writers were convinced that lions preyed on mostly old or sick animals, or vulnerable youngsters. Most of the recent studies dispel this theory. Lions take disadvantaged animals when they are available, but they are just as likely to take animals who are in their prime. One of the exceptions, however, concerns buffalo cows, calves and yearlings, which are taken in proportion to their occurrence in the population, whereas prime adult bulls are seldom killed. Old bulls that have left the herd are taken quite frequently. Whilst the hunting technique of wild dogs, for example, allows them to probe and test their potential prey for weaknesses, so that they take more old or sick animals, lions employ different means when hunting. Lions take care in stalking their prey, and usually end up taking the closest animal – regardless of its age, sex or condition. Undoubtedly the seasons have an influence on the age of the prey taken; for example, more wildebeest calves or impala lambs are killed during the summer months when these species have experienced their seasonal birth peaks.

In many antelope species a preponderance of males are found in lion kills. Males comprise about 60 per cent of kills from areas as distinct as Kafue, Kruger and East Africa. As most antelope have an adult sex ratio favouring females, this indicates either selectivity on the part of the lions, or it may suggest that adult male antelopes are more vulnerable to attack by lions. One explanation for this phenomenon may be that male antelopes have a shorter flight distance; that is, they stand their ground longer than the more cautious females, and thus they are more often killed. Some biologists argue that territorial males are more vulnerable to lions, but the evidence does not support this proposition. It would appear, rather, that bachelor males who have not yet established themselves, and older males who have lost their territories to stronger animals, are the most vulnerable – because they have access only to poorer habitat.

It stands to reason that territorial males occupy better terrain, one of the main features of which will be the greater safety it affords from predators.

In the case of most animals, equal numbers of males and females are born. Thereafter, there are mechanisms that come into play causing differential mortality which result in male populations being reduced. Males need to fight for dominance, and because they are larger-bodied than females, they have greater energy requirements. As most of the ungulates have social systems in which individual males may mate with several or many females, there is usually a surplus of adult males. If these are taken by lions it is not harmful to the population, provided also that territory-holding males are displaced occasionally by youngsters.

✳

The lion's physical evolution and behaviour has been formed by the requirements of the hunt. As mentioned earlier, it has been hypothesized that the social structure of lions is based on the need for cooperative hunting. Some scientists, however, have argued that cooperative hunting is a consequence, rather than a cause, of group living. Data which shows solitary lions achieving a higher rate of food intake than lions forming part of a pride certainly indicate that the advantage of group living does not lie in having access to the pride's food supply.

The hunting procedure consists of several components, and it can be argued that each component is enhanced by the participation of more than one animal. To begin with the lion must locate the prey, then approach and stalk it. This is followed by the chase, the capture, and the kill. Finding food is the motivation for the hunt and, if success is achieved, food is also the reward.

Lions hunt primarily by sight. Although their sense of smell and their hearing assist in alerting them to the whereabouts of prey animals, visual cues trigger the hunt. Most hunting is done under the poor light conditions of early

Opposite: Nomadic young adults often wander over large areas in search of a territory and females. Left: The scars on the nose of an old male lion indicate that he has survived many territorial battles – and proved himself fit to hold females and father cubs.

ungulates. This idea has since been tested by generations of modern biologists and, largely, it has been found wanting. Food availability, and the presence of parasites and disease pose a far greater threat to the survival of antelope and other ungulates than do predators.

There are certain situations, however, in which lions may have some influence on their prey populations. Usually these circumstances are the result of intervention by humans – such as the introduction of a new species into an area, or the creation of man-made waterholes in arid areas, where lions are then able to ambush their prey more easily. Under natural conditions there are no known incidents of lions detrimentally affecting prey populations.

There are many facets to the role of lions as predators in any given eco-system. There is the relationship of lion numbers to the abundance of potential prey in an area; whether they hunt selectively for particular species, sex or age groups; whether they take old or infirm animals or young and fit animals; what numbers of animals they remove from a system; and seasonal changes in their prey selection. All are fundamental to any understanding of this great cat's role on the African savanna.

Many biologists have looked for a rule-of-thumb predator : prey ratio, which might indicate how many lions a given area with a known number of game animals can support. The process of arriving at such a figure is always complicated by aspects such as the differences in size of the various species comprising a prey community, lions' preference for a particular species, as well as prey vulnerability and availability (that is, the ease with which they can be taken). Scientists have published figures of 1:100 for Hwange in Zimbabwe; 1:126 for Nairobi; 1:103 for the Kruger National Park, 1:174 for Manyara, 1:275 for the Serengeti and 1:88 for Etosha in Namibia. Generally, the best estimate is that any game area requires well over 100 game animals to support one lion through the course of a year. Since lions are at the top of the food pyramid, they clearly require a wide base of prey species below them.

No fixed figure can be given for the number of prey animals killed by a lion in one year. Estimates vary from 10 to 36, but these can only have general validity as factors such as the the individual lion's size, sex, and, if it was a female, whether she was lactating or pregnant, would all have an influence. An individual adult male lion can consume over 40 kilograms of meat at a sitting, but it can then go for many days without eating. An adult female in the wild consumes about five kilograms of meat a day. Statistics obtained from the diet of zoo lions, which require four to seven kilograms of meat daily, are misleading because they apply to animals who are generally rather inactive and therefore have low energy requirements. Diets designed by a zoo are also likely to be more nutritious than the diet of a lion in the wild, as zoo lions often receive their meat sprinkled with various vitamin and mineral supplements.

In times gone by, many nature writers were convinced that lions preyed on mostly old or sick animals, or vulnerable youngsters. Most of the recent studies dispel this theory. Lions take disadvantaged animals when they are available, but they are just as likely to take animals who are in their prime. One of the exceptions, however, concerns buffalo cows, calves and yearlings, which are taken in proportion to their occurrence in the population, whereas prime adult bulls are seldom killed. Old bulls that have left the herd are taken quite frequently. Whilst the hunting technique of wild dogs, for example, allows them to probe and test their potential prey for weaknesses, so that they take more old or sick animals, lions employ different means when hunting. Lions take care in stalking their prey, and usually end up taking the closest animal – regardless of its age, sex or condition. Undoubtedly the seasons have an influence on the age of the prey taken; for example, more wildebeest calves or impala lambs are killed during the summer months when these species have experienced their seasonal birth peaks.

In many antelope species a preponderance of males are found in lion kills. Males comprise about 60 per cent of kills from areas as distinct as Kafue, Kruger and East Africa. As most antelope have an adult sex ratio favouring females, this indicates either selectivity on the part of the lions, or it may suggest that adult male antelopes are more vulnerable to attack by lions. One explanation for this phenomenon may be that male antelopes have a shorter flight distance; that is, they stand their ground longer than the more cautious females, and thus they are more often killed. Some biologists argue that territorial males are more vulnerable to lions, but the evidence does not support this proposition. It would appear, rather, that bachelor males who have not yet established themselves, and older males who have lost their territories to stronger animals, are the most vulnerable – because they have access only to poorer habitat.

It stands to reason that territorial males occupy better terrain, one of the main features of which will be the greater safety it affords from predators.

In the case of most animals, equal numbers of males and females are born. Thereafter, there are mechanisms that come into play causing differential mortality which result in male populations being reduced. Males need to fight for dominance, and because they are larger-bodied than females, they have greater energy requirements. As most of the ungulates have social systems in which individual males may mate with several or many females, there is usually a surplus of adult males. If these are taken by lions it is not harmful to the population, provided also that territory-holding males are displaced occasionally by youngsters.

✳

The lion's physical evolution and behaviour has been formed by the requirements of the hunt. As mentioned earlier, it has been hypothesized that the social structure of lions is based on the need for cooperative hunting. Some scientists, however, have argued that cooperative hunting is a consequence, rather than a cause, of group living. Data which shows solitary lions achieving a higher rate of food intake than lions forming part of a pride certainly indicate that the advantage of group living does not lie in having access to the pride's food supply.

The hunting procedure consists of several components, and it can be argued that each component is enhanced by the participation of more than one animal. To begin with the lion must locate the prey, then approach and stalk it. This is followed by the chase, the capture, and the kill. Finding food is the motivation for the hunt and, if success is achieved, food is also the reward.

Lions hunt primarily by sight. Although their sense of smell and their hearing assist in alerting them to the whereabouts of prey animals, visual cues trigger the hunt. Most hunting is done under the poor light conditions of early

If they are lucky they end up in a protected area – most, however, are killed.

In late 1987 the wanderings of a nomadic lion were recorded in Namibia. Researchers were able to piece together the movements – over a period of two months – of a five-year-old male with a distinctive spoor caused by an injury. The lion covered a distance of about 500 kilometres between the Ugab and Kuiseb rivers in the central Namib Desert. Along the way he killed two cows and a donkey, and his adventure only ended when he was captured by game rangers and moved to the Skeleton Coast Park, where he was fitted with a radio-transmitter collar before being released.

✳

Like other cats, lions adapt well to the particular circumstances in which they find themselves. They select their prey from the spectrum of available animals, but, given a choice, usually exhibit a definite preference for large ungulates. It has been argued that the social structure of lions has evolved from the necessity of cooperation in bringing down such large animals successfully.

Most studies have shown that lions' prey falls in the weight range of 20 to 800 kilograms in mass. This wide spectrum effectively includes warthog and gazelle at the lower end of the scale, and animals such as giraffe and Cape buffalo at the upper end. Occasionally lions in groups may attack and kill even heavier animals such as black rhinoceros, white rhinoceros and hippopotamus, but this is not the norm. Lions also take small animals, such as springhares and steenbok, and records show that Kalahari and Kruger lions regularly kill porcupines. This kind of prey animal is too small to contribute a major part to a lion's food intake, though, and it is unlikely that a pride would thrive and raise cubs on such meagre fare. Such small animals may, however, be used to tide lions over during hard times, especially in areas where larger game migrate and are therefore not always readily available.

The role of lions in a savanna ecosystem has long been a point of debate when planning wildlife management strategies for national parks in Africa. Early in the twentieth century many of these parks followed a blanket anti-predator policy. This meant that rangers shot lions and other predators on sight, believing that ungulates would then stand a better chance of survival.

In the years between 1902 and 1946, during the reign of the pioneering warden Lt Col Stevenson-Hamilton, thousands of lions were shot in South Africa's Kruger National Park. At the time it was assumed that lions and other predators were the main mechanism of population regulation acting upon

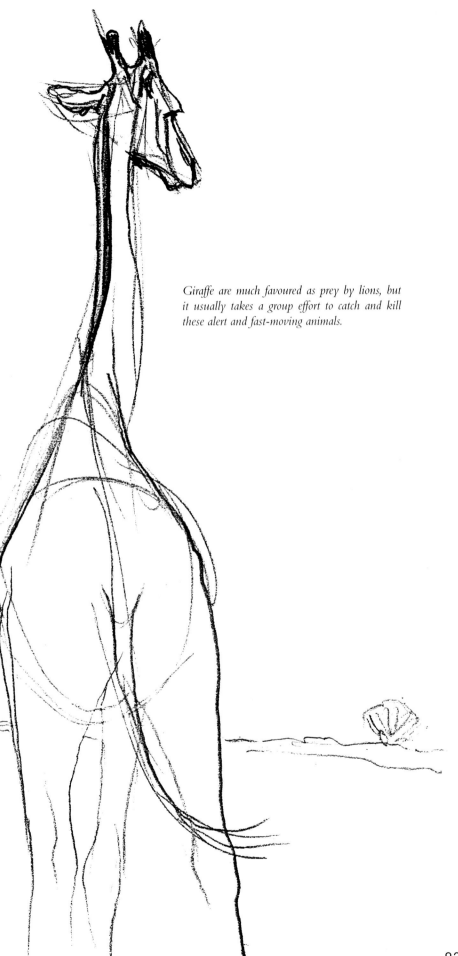

Giraffe are much favoured as prey by lions, but it usually takes a group effort to catch and kill these alert and fast-moving animals.

83

Left: Antelope form the bulk of the lion's diet in Africa – yet predation has little impact on their numbers. Of far more consequence are starvation, parasites and disease.
Below: Even the tsessebe – fleetest of all antelope – is occasionally ambushed and killed by lions.

evening or dawn, and during the night. As a lion's hunting technique depends on a stalk to get within range of its prey, it is at a disadvantage during daylight when prey animals themselves are better able to see. The lion's final charge is usually made from as close as 10 metres and seldom exceeds 20 metres.

When hunting, the pride usually walks along in a fairly loose formation. Sometimes they may fan out, and sometimes they move in single file. Individuals occasionally detour to investigate an area, then return to the general direction of the group's movement. During this phase of the hunt there may be some audible communication between members of the pride, with lionesses making low grunts or humming coughs to maintain contact with their cubs. The body postures of individuals, however, are far more important means of communication at this time. During their search for prey, lions saunter casually with their heads up. Occasionally they sit on their haunches looking around, and sometimes they flop down alone or

with a companion to rest for a moment before continuing their walkabout.

The instant potential prey is sighted by a lioness, she immediately freezes or sinks down into cover, staring intently at the prey – her ears cocked and her tail held perfectly still, or just its tip moving slowly from side to side. The other lions quickly take note of her changed posture and also attempt to locate the prey. The careful stalk begins as the lioness moves, holding her body low, muscles bulging and rippling along her powerful shoulders. She seems to glide over the ground with her head stretching forward, still with ears cocked – their black tips serving as beacons to those following – and her eyes riveted on the quarry. Her progress may be rapid or slow; she may give a few quick paces and then freeze – even in mid stride – with one paw off the ground. Every possible scrap of cover is exploited: termite mounds, trees, small bushes, or even clumps of grass behind which a full-grown lioness can literally seem to melt away.

Both Paul and I have watched the build-up to a kill on several occasions, but the sense of drama never dulls. I remember one instance particularly well. The stalk had gone well and the lioness was close enough to attack. She paused, gathering her hind legs under her body slowly and with great care, preparing to spring. She moved her front paws to gain firm footing, while her eyes remained glued to her prey – a grazing wildebeest. Unaware of the approaching danger, the antelope turned to lick its shoulder, and then lifted its head to gaze into the distance at a rival parading on his dung heap.

Soundlessly the cat burst from cover, her powerful limbs driving her forward. Within two seconds she had covered the ground between herself and her prey, and grabbed the wildebeest across the shoulder, gripping its body with her claws. There was no escape – her paw raked into the bull's neck and, like a vice, her jaws clamped over its muzzle. Locked in the struggle, both hunter and hunted tumbled to the ground in a cloud of dust.

The lioness's rush instantly triggered the help of

her companions, who sped in from the flanks. In a trice, another lioness had the wildebeest by the shoulders, holding its writhing body down with her weight, but keeping well away from the flailing hooves. The suffocating grip on the nose and mouth soon did its work and in a minute or two the animal was dead. By now the rest of the pride had joined in.

Lions are extremely powerful – they can grab and throw a fully grown zebra using only a grip on its rump. Using a forepaw to deliver a heavy blow to the head of an antelope is probably sufficient to stun the animal. The lion's most frequently used technique for dispatching antelopes, however, is the suffocating hold on the muzzle. Sometimes, though, the lion will latch onto the throat of its prey, the hardness of the trachea prolonging the killing process. Usually the killing is clean and quick, with little biting or tearing at the prey taking place. Things can go wrong, of course, like when a lioness misses her grip, or in a case where an animal such as a buffalo, sable antelope bull or adult hippo puts up a good fight. Occasionally, a lion will hit an animal on the shoulder or jump on its back, using a forepaw to pull the prey's muzzle sharply up and back as it falls. This technique can break the prey animal's neck, killing it instantly.

There has been much debate over the degree of coordination shown between members of a hunting pride, and their levels of communication and planning. Many reports describe how some members of a pride stay hidden behind cover while their colleagues circle the chosen prey and drive it toward the ambush. Some of the reports credit lions with a fine grasp of strategy, even suggesting that they are capable of circling upwind, deliberately causing the prey to rush away downwind into a trap. One such story, heard at my father's knee, told of a lion circling upwind of a cattle kraal or stockade, then deliberately urinating to give the cattle his scent, thus panicking them into breaking out of the kraal and dashing off downwind into the dark – into the ambush of other lions. Such stories seldom stand up to critical scrutiny and usually the incidents can be explained on the basis of a very loosely organized hunt with individual lions acting independently and simply taking advantage of the situation that may develop.

What is important, is mutual assistance in handling a struggling animal and in the teamwork needed to attack a large, dangerous animal like a buffalo. Even if some of the hunters do no more than distract the prey to allow other lions to get in close or to leap onto the buffalo's back without being gored, they contribute to the hunt's success. The situation requires a dead buffalo, but not at the cost of an injured lion. In large prides some females may not always participate in a hunt, only assisting when large or dangerous prey is being tackled and staying aloof when smaller species are taken.

Over countless generations, lions have evolved special techniques to overcome the not inconsiderable defences or weapons of certain prey animals. The Kalahari gemsbok, or Cape oryx, for example, is a very dangerous animal. It is extremely brave when brought to bay and fully able to kill a lion with its rapier-like horns. Lions know this and will not tackle a gemsbok head-on – if they cannot approach the antelope unseen from behind, they will leave it alone. Generally lions can only down a gemsbok by biting through its neck or spine; after immobilizing the animal in this way, they then go for the vulnerable throat to ensure a quick kill.

The practised technique for killing giraffe is also highly specialized. The key is to knock the lanky animal off its feet, pulling it down without getting in the way of the hooves of its powerful front feet, which can be used to chop at the lion with dangerous accuracy. The hind legs are also formidable weapons as the giraffe is able to kick backwards like a zebra, using one foot at a time or both feet together, even kicking forwards or sideways on occasion.

Lions don't always have an easy time

Opposite: Alert to signs of danger, a subadult Buffon's kob stares at a lion in the distance in the Niokolo-Koba National Park of Senegal.
Left: The telltale swishing of the tail from side to side is part of the body language of a lioness preparing for a chase.

killing dangerous game and frequently suffer injuries. When an injury is temporary, such as a muscular injury or sprain, the pride system offers support until the lion recovers. The injured lion is allowed to feed from the pride's kills, though it may temporarily be unable to hunt. In the case of an injured mother, her cubs may suckle from other lionesses until she recovers.

Lions can be injured by lesser animals, as well as by the well-recognized dangerous quarries such as buffalo. A well-placed kick from a zebra, a slashing warthog tusk, or even a tearing kick from an ostrich can do great damage. The most dangerous kick from a zebra is that which hits a lion in the face, breaking a jaw or removing an eye. Kicks to the chest or body are generally less serious.

The porcupine is a small animal, and much favoured by lions, but it quite literally carries a sting in its tail. Contrary to popular legend the needle-sharp porcupine quills are not shot at a predator, instead the mobile tail of the porcupine is used to swat at the source of danger. As a result, many a lion has ended up with quills embedded in an incautious paw or nose. Also, if a lion bites at a porcupine, it can get quills stuck in its mouth. I remember seeing a lioness in a truly terrible condition in the southern Kalahari. She had two short porcupine quills embedded in her palate and tongue, forcing her mouth into an open position. She could neither eat nor drink, and died as a result.

Buffalo and sable antelope are pugnacious animals and will put up a deter-mined fight if attacked by a lion. We once watched spellbound as a lioness took a buffalo calf from a herd and wrestled it to the ground. The calf's mother, noticing the plight of her offspring, turned and charged the lioness, using her horns to toss the offending cat into the air. Somehow the lioness maintained her hold on the calf, but the enraged cow was not done and attacked again. The lioness landed heavily on her back, losing her grip on the calf in the process. By this stage the cat had had enough, and it ran for cover. The calf appeared none the worse for its ordeal and within moments had recovered sufficiently to scuttle off safely behind its mother. On another occasion I witnessed a lion making a rush toward a herd of buffalo, only

to stop dead in his tracks when half a dozen of the big black animals firmly stood their ground and turned to face him.

Occasionally lions encounter a herd of weakened or confused animals and may slaughter far more than they can ever hope to eat. Observers have seen lions entering cattle pens and killing numerous animals. This rarely happens in the wild, but there is one record from the Kruger National Park in which 15 buffalo were killed by a pride of lions during a single attack. Only a few of the buffalo were devoured. During the severe drought of 1985 in the Kalahari, thousands of eland, wildebeest and other animals died, and many more antelope wandered around in a weakened state. Lions would lie in wait for these vulnerable beasts at waterholes, and then launch themselves at the group, killing several at a time. Already satiated, the lions would take only a few bites, leaving the bulk of the carcasses to rot. Such killing frenzies are known in other carnivores as well, and it appears that once the impulse to kill has been stimulated, it continues unabated in the presence of so many vulnerable targets.

Lions often move their prey from the killing ground to a sheltered spot nearby. During the day this allows the lions to feed in the shade, and it also keeps the carcass out of the sight of vultures, whose attendance might attract other lions or hyaenas. If the prey is a small animal the carcass may be carried off in the lion's mouth, but a heavier prey animal is usually taken by the neck and then dragged off by a lion straddling it. Other members of the pride are as likely to hinder as they are to help, as they may attempt to drag the carcass in a different direction or try to start feeding. Young cubs, with their innate youthful exuberance, may latch onto a kill and be dragged along with it. The heaviest of carcasses, buffaloes and giraffes for example, cannot be pulled along in this manner. The carcass will, instead, be pulled along by a lion walking backwards to gain maximum purchase with all four legs, or by several lions working in concert.

The distance over which a carcass is dragged by a lion may be up to approximately 400 metres, but if suitable shelter is to hand the journey is seldom more than about 50 metres. The lions of Namibia's Skeleton Coast, however, are often faced with a particularly arduous task. In this remote area, where the unforgiving desert landscape is frequently fogbound and scoured by cold, howling winds whipping up stinging sandstorms, lions have been known to drag Cape fur seal carcasses for up to 2.6 kilometres to the shelter of hummocks or reed beds.

Above: Although it does show some superficial similarities to the Cape buffalo, the blue wildebeest is in fact an antelope quite closely related to impala and hartebeest.
Opposite: The wildebeest makes a final defiant stand – with the odds in favour of the cat.

Lions may eat the intestines, but seldom touch the stomach. The lion may sometimes gut its prey on the spot before dragging it away to feed. Gutting is done by first hooking a canine through the belly of the prey to make way for the carnassial teeth – formidable shearing tools easily able to slice through the soft skin. The lion will then rip the guts out, sometimes covering it with dirt and leaves. The theory is that this behaviour is an evolutionary throwback to earlier times, when lions would cover a carcass, leaving it to return later to feed. Lions no longer do this, and it is unlikely that they would ever have done so in the African environment where there has never been a lack of scavengers to dispose of any unattended remains. If the lions' ancestors hailed from Europe's forests as is suggested by some scientists, however, they may not have had to deal with such fierce competition.

Lionesses and cubs begin feeding on the internal organs – heart, liver, kidneys and lungs. Male lions are more likely to start feeding on the hind-quarters. Usually the animal that made the kill appears exhausted or highly excited by its efforts, and will lie down and rest next to the carcass, or pace about in an agitated manner for some time. The rest of the pride show no such restraint, however, and in the initial rush to feed there is much growling, snarling, snapping and swatting at one another as pride members vie to get their fill. The context of this situation may explain why, in its highly charged, adrenalin-boosted state, the killer only joins in later when it has calmed down.

Paul Bosman -76

Left: Vultures appear very quickly once a kill has been made. Gathering from vast distances, they drop out of the sky to perch in trees and patiently wait their turn.
Right: A pride will be aware of vultures waiting to move in on a kill, but whilst the lions are feeding, scavengers will keep their distance.

In the melée which ensues, cubs and youngsters are sometimes injured by adults, especially by males competing aggressively for a feeding site around the carcass. It would be a foolish mother, therefore, that would allow her small cubs to enter the fray. Notwithstanding this, however, males sometimes tolerate young cubs trying to feed whilst, at the same time, keeping their mother away – presumably the males do not regard the small cubs as serious competitors. More often, though, it is only once the adults have withdrawn from a carcass that the youngsters and cubs are free to nibble at scraps, gnaw bones, lick up blood and hone their feeding skills in general.

Lions are the only cats that habitually feed whilst lying on their bellies – most other cats sit, crouch or stand when feeding. Lions are also adept at using their forepaws to hold down the carcass whilst they tear and pull at it. Feeding progresses from the body cavity and hindquarters to the ribs and limbs, leaving the neck and head until last. The softer bones, such as ribs, are crunched and chewed; long

bones are gnawed and licked clean of meat by the lions' rasp-like tongues. The thick ribs of animals such as buffalo and giraffe are licked, with only their ends being chewed. In the case of a small animal, for example a wildebeest calf, most of the bones are consumed, with only the head, feet and part of the vertebral column being left as pickings for scavengers. Impala or springbok lambs are eaten hooves and all.

A pride of lions may take three or four days to finish off a large buffalo or giraffe. In the Kasungu National Park in Malawi we once observed two males spending a week at the carcass of an eight-year-old elephant they had killed. During the course of the day the lions took turns guarding the remains, chasing off jackals, hyaenas and vultures. The off-duty animal would rest in the shade, walk to a nearby stream for a drink and then return to relieve his companion. As the carcass was lying in the open and was too heavy to move, the lion on guard had no respite from heat, thirst or flies for hours on end. Vultures, which sat patiently in the surrounding trees, were eventually rewarded when the two bloated lions moved off, leaving behind the elephant's remains and their temporary latrine consisting of huge blobs of sticky, smelly, black faeces.

Right: Lions waste no time at all in starting their meal. The noise of a kill can travel far, and it can easily attract unwelcome guests like scavenging spotted hyaenas, which will have to be seen off.

When water is available lions drink regularly, particularly when it is hot, but they don't invest much in the activity and seldom take more than a few minutes to drink their fill. They are not fastidious about the quality of water and will drink from pools, rivers or waterholes, showing little indication of preference. Drinking is a social event, often taking place after feeding when the pride tends to move to water en masse, usually crowding together at the water's edge in a manner reminiscent of the close contact maintained during feeding.

✳

Most interactions between lions and humans occurring today are limited to encounters in game reserves. In areas with high-density tourist traffic, lions have become habituated to the passage of vehicles and hardly display any reaction at all. There are numerous records of lions stalking game from behind the cover of cars and buses, or settling down to rest in the shade provided by these vehicles. Such 'park' lions offer visitors wonderful opportunities of watching them for hours as the huge cats do what they do best – lie around and rest, whilst looking majestic.

Most game reserves require vehicles to stay on roads or tracks, so lions can easily avoid people if they wish to. In the densely wooded southern African parks, such as the Kruger National Park, lions need go no more than a few metres to be totally hidden from view. In privately owned game reserves like Mala Mala, which lies adjacent to Kruger, or Mashatu in Botswana, guests are taken on safari drives in open vehicles which can travel cross-country to follow hunting lions. With the aid of powerful spotlights, to which the lions quickly grow accustomed, the safari guides also follow nocturnal hunts and observe the kills taking place.

In more remote areas of the large parks like Kruger and Botswana's Gemsbok National Park, or smaller parks with less traffic like Niokolo-Koba in Senegal, lions tend to be less trusting of vehicles and may move off quickly when approached. Alternatively, they may freeze at the first sound of an approaching vehicle, and only move off once eye contact has been established. They may move away gradually with a slow, steady retreat, or at a run if they are nervous. In safari-hunting areas lions are wary of humans and avoid contact wherever possible.

Left: The rapier-like horns of the Cape oryx are formidable weapons in a frontal attack.
Right: Confident of their strength and numbers, a gathering of Cape buffalo bulls shows little concern at the close approach of a solitary lion.

In many remote areas stock-killing lions are today dealt with by using gun-traps, and by leaving a dead cow or donkey as bait. Although they are now relatively seldom found in Africa, gin traps or spring traps were stock in trade at any small country store or trading post in the earlier years of this century. The traps came in various sizes – small ones for catching jackals, medium-sized ones for trapping leopards and large ones for lions – and they were deadly. This fact may explain why they are no longer so common, as they were used to clear large areas of Africa of its predators, and are therefore now no longer needed.

Another effective way of dealing with stock-killing lions was using bait laced with strychnine – one of the deadliest of poisons. This was a simple way of killing not only lions, but many other predators and scavengers, including vultures and bateleurs. Strychnine was widely used at one time and was issued by government authorities to anyone complaining of stock losses. Today lions are largely confined to remote, uninhabited or protected areas and there is a low incidence of livestock killing.

African literature abounds with stories of man-eating lions and many rural areas have, at some time or another, been notorious for harbouring man-eaters. In Kenya the best-known saga concerned the lions of Tsavo which made a name for themselves at the turn of the century by killing workers on the railway between Mombasa and Nairobi. These lions brought construction work to a complete standstill, and it was only after they had been dispatched by Colonel Patterson, a well-known hunter of the time, that work could be resumed.

Man-eating is not as prevalent today as it may have been in the past, but it still occurs. As recently as the 1970s the Namweras and Kasupe districts of Malawi had a reputation for harbouring man-eating lions. These lions turned to man-eating largely as a result of the increase in the human population and the subsequent decline of the game population. Especially during the rainy season, when wild animals were widely dispersed and not so readily accessible to lions, humans became targets. When lions came across people, especially people sleeping outdoors at night, they took them. They also took dogs, goats, pigs and other livestock. The lions were not necessarily old or injured – just hungry. It is true, however, that those lions turning to humans as a source of prey are often found to be old or injured and no longer able to cope with their usual quarry. In the past decade there have been two incidents involving man-eating lions in the Kruger National Park, and a man-killer was recently found at Santawani in the Okavango Delta of Botswana.

National parks remain the lion's most important refuges. As these havens become increasingly developed for tourism or become more intensively managed (as is presently the case in southern Africa), intensive management of the lion populations they harbour is not far off. In the Hluhluwe-Umfolozi Park in KwaZulu-Natal, a reintroduced lion population is carefully controlled.

Various alternative solutions to culling have been explored. In the Etosha National Park, for example, the problems with lions are complex and relate to a range of consequences of human interference with the natural system which have significantly altered the area's predator–prey balance. Etosha, like so many other protected areas, has artificial boundaries. Erecting fences around the park in order to reduce wildlife–livestock conflicts had a major impact on the age-old migration routes used by wildebeest, zebra and springbok – the lion's natural prey. The migrations were determined largely by rainfall and hence by available water. To counter the loss of dry-season areas of game concentration, boreholes were drilled inside the park to provide permanent water in areas which had previously been used only seasonally.

A further impact of park development originated from the numerous gravel pits that were created to supply road-building material. These gravel pits filled with water during the rainy season and became ideal incubation areas for anthrax, a deadly bacterial disease. Although lions are immune to this disease, ungulates are not. Thus game that drank from the infected pits either became diseased and died of their own accord, or, in their weakened state, became easy prey for lions. These plentiful 'waterholes' also provided additional places of ambush which the lions quickly exploited.

For lions the outcome of all these changes to the system was lower cub mortality and a consequent increase in numbers. The predator:prey ratio changed to about 1:72–105. The wildebeest population started to decline under this intense predation pressure. In addition, it was shown that the increase in lion numbers was accompanied by a drastic decline in the populations of other predators such as cheetahs, spotted hyaenas and wild dogs.

A simple solution to this man-induced situation would have been to cull the lions, thus pushing the predator:prey ratio closer to the values recorded elsewhere. However, Etosha decided to exercise some other options. Closing down boreholes in the central areas of the park started changing wildebeest migrations back toward the original pattern. Innovative research into the use

Left: Four lionesses gather around their kill, a full-grown Cape buffalo cow, the half-digested contents of the rumen first having been removed and dragged to the side.
Right: Though incapable of killing an adult elephant themselves, lions will readily scavenge from the abundant supply of food it offers.
Below: When the lions and scavengers have had their fill, there is little left of a once huge and proud Cape buffalo bull.

An example of the kind of dilemma faced in managing lion populations is deciding what to do when subadult lions are driven out of a pride, or leave the pride of their own accord to become nomads. Their resultant wanderings invariably take them out of the reserve onto surrounding tribal land where there is little or no game. There they then take to killing cattle, and have to be destroyed. To forestall this situation, which understandably antagonizes the communities involved, these subadult lions are culled inside the reserve before they venture out to cause problems. This is a harsh but prudent policy.

kills was based largely on information supplied in the form of regular field reports by game rangers. Much of this data, however, resulted from interpreting spoor and evidence at a kill long after it had happened, and sometimes long after the lions had departed. By its very nature, the data gathered in this way tended to centre around information on lion predation with respect to large game animals, as these kills were often brought to the rangers' attention by gatherings of vultures and other scavengers. Only large kills would draw vultures for more than a day, so evidence of lion kills on small animals remained unrecorded for the most part.

George Schaller, on the other hand, spent some years during the late 1960s working on the largely open plains of the Serengeti National Park in Tanzania. Here he followed lion prides on the hunt and recorded not only their successes, but also their many failures. He could identify his study animals and accumulated records of their kills over extended periods of time. Many other researchers throughout Africa also used these methods to accumulate data on the role of lion predation and social behaviour in African ecosystems.

Researchers working in small areas, like Judith Rudnai who studied the lions of Kenya's Nairobi National Park, have been able to identify each individual in a given lion population. From such intimate knowledge researchers could gather more information on social interactions among individual lions and data on the survival of cubs. When lions could not be easily identified, researchers marked their study animals using ear tags, colour-coded collars, brand marks burned into the skin and ear tattoos. The application of these marking techniques was made possible by advances in the chemical immobilization of wild animals. This achievement was a highlight of African wildlife science in the early 1970s.

Dr Butch Smuts and his colleagues in the Kruger National Park spent several years studying lions, and perfected a mass-capture technique. In addition to investigating the ecology of lions, they wanted to take

of contraception in the lion population became another option.

Some very important studies in lion contraception were conducted by Dr Jock Orford, a gynaecologist, and Dr Hu Berry, a biologist working in the park. A total of 10 lionesses were darted. When the immobilizing drugs took effect, synthetic hormone capsules were implanted in the lionesses. The capsules slowly release a drug into the bloodstream, inhibiting the animals' oestrous cycle and preventing ovulation for up to five years.

This kind of birth control has many advantages as a method for curbing the increase in the lion population, and there is a strong ethical argument for reversible contraception versus irreversible killing. Contraception can be terminated at any time simply by removing the hormone capsule. In addition, the lionesses' genes are not lost to the lion population, as they would have been if they had merely been shot.

As the lion is the top predator in any African ecosystem in which it occurs, it has attracted the attention of research scientists for many years. Pioneering studies were carried out by people like Dr Tol Pienaar and Dr George Schaller. From the late 1950s Tol Pienaar worked as a biologist in the Kruger National Park, where his interest in lions centred on their role as predators and the impact of predation on ungulate populations. His data on lion

Opposite, above: As the number of lions at a carcass diminishes, the scavengers gather courage from their own numbers and cautiously approach, eager for the scraps that are still left.
Above: The lion is an integral part of the image of African savanna – as characteristic as the flat-topped umbrella thorn or the ilala palm.
Below: After feeding, lions make their way to water to drink, and then to rest, amply satisfied.

Above: Many game species, like these impala, move to waterholes to drink in the heat of the day. Right: A courting male lion is in attendance on the female of his choice for her entire oestrous period – a devoted and constant companion.

an accurate census of lions in the heavily wooded savanna of the Kruger National Park. The density of the vegetation prevented the lions from being easily followed and immobilized as they had been in the case of the Serengeti. Therefore, the researchers polished techniques used by hunters to lure lions to bait, where they would then dart all the members of the pride. They discovered that they could call lions to bait by playing amplified tape recordings of the growling and snarling sounds made by feeding lions at a kill; the excited 'laughing' calls of scavenging spotted hyaenas; and the occasional yelping calls of black-backed jackals. Playing recordings of lions' roaring sounds tended to discourage lions from approaching the bait. To reinforce the illusion of a kill nearby, the researchers also dragged the carcass of the bait animal from various points along roads and tracks to the capture site, where the carcass was then firmly chained to a tree.

The bait was positioned just before sunset in order to coincide with the lions' natural nocturnal activities. Calling was initiated soon after dark. The research team would wait in a hide about 20 paces from the bait. When the lions had settled on the bait and started feeding, they were exposed to gradually lengthening bursts of light from a battery-powered spotlight. At first the lions reacted instantly, jumping up and dashing off to a position a few paces beyond the reach of the light beam. They quickly became conditioned, however, especially if they were hungry. Soon they would carry on feeding at ease in the spotlight's glare. Then the researchers would begin darting the animals. The marksman's target was the heavily muscled area on the lion's shoulder or rump. A lion being hit by a dart would usually jump up, but its companions would continue feeding, hardly perturbed. The spotlight was turned off for a few seconds after each shot so that the other lions would not be disturbed

by the sight of the dart. The process was repeated until all the lions gathered at the bait had been darted.

As soon as the immobilizing drug started taking an effect, the darted lions would become highly lethargic. They would try to continue chewing at the bait, but would become increasingly drowsy and disoriented. The final sign of anaesthesia was a gradual enlargement of the pupils as the lions became unable to coordinate their vision or limbs and fell into a deep sleep. Once all the lions had become immobile, they were approached cautiously and checked. Then they were measured, weighed, examined and marked, while details of their age and sex were recorded. When all the procedures had been completed the lions were placed in a suitable spot and left to recover. It took some hours for the effects of the drug to wear off, allowing the lions to wake slowly and regain coordination. Many lions resumed feeding as soon as they could walk to the carcass – others would lie and rest for several hours.

The work in Kruger was a great success. A total of 971 lions were lured to the capture sites and, of these, 775 were captured and 550 marked. As many as 21 lions were captured per night. The capture technique was later also used in the Kalahari Gemsbok National Park for a similar census. Comparable techniques for capture and marking of large numbers of lions were used elsewhere in southern and East Africa.

Dr Hu Berry modified the mass-capture technique to enable him to mark and study lions in the arid environment of Etosha. As the vegetation of Etosha is far less dense than Kruger's, it is possible to track and dart lions easily during daylight. Darting lions by day in the Etosha environment, however, required researchers to pay attention to a number of factors that did not come into play at night. The pupils of an immobilized lion dilate considerably, so special care was taken to ensure that the eyes remained moist and free of infection. A blindfold was also applied to the animal to protect its eyes from the harsh daylight. Daytime temperatures in Etosha are high, so particular attention was paid to the lions' respiration, heartbeat and body temperature. Lions pant to dissipate body heat and, when it is hot, they may pant at a rate of up to 140 times a minute. When a lion is anaesthetized, the breathing rate drops to about 15 pants a minute and the deep body temperature rises quickly. Lions were therefore handled in the shade, but also sprayed with cold water occasionally to prevent high body temperatures. The Etosha lions were also weighed, measured and marked for long-term observation. The studies have since been carried out by day and by night, with every aspect of lion behaviour and activity being monitored. To obtain accurate information on lions' nocturnal activities an image intensifier has been used to observe them on moonless nights.

More recently, radio telemetry has simplified research on lion movement, population densities, social interactions within and between groups, dispersal and population dynamics. Radio-collared lions can be followed even in densely bushed environments, thus allowing an accurate recording of kills and interactions between lion prides. The collars are manufactured from machine belting or other durable materials and the radio transmitter is sealed in a waterproof capsule attached to the collar. The life span of the transmitter is determined by the size and number of batteries, and by the characteristics of the signal it emits. Slow, regularly spaced beats use less power than rapid beats. The signals can be traced by observers on foot, in vehicles or in aircraft. The results of such studies are now available in scientific literature and from them it is possible to piece together a remarkably accurate picture of the African lion's life under different environmental conditions.

A fascinating study on the ecology of lions, by Professor Fritz Eloff, has been continuing in the Kalahari Gemsbok National Park for over 30 years. This study is special not only due to its duration, but because it depends on no modern technology – apart from a vehicle – for collecting data. It depends, instead, upon the skill of San trackers who interpret the life of the Kalahari lion from its spoor. Whereas most other scientists have studied lions at their kills – and thereby recorded only the successful kills, and mostly the large animals killed – Eloff and his San helpers have been able to follow the tracks of lions for days on end, recording all the details of their wanderings and hunts.

Right: The amazing agility of a young impala, and its ability to dart and leap at speed, protect it from predation.
Far right: The helmeted or crowned guinea fowl is one of Africa's most ubiquitous ground birds found just about everywhere except in equatorial forests.

Opposite: The sexual dimorphism of lions, with adult males being distinctly different and larger than females, may be linked to their social lifestyle. Above: The favoured habitat of the African lion varies from open grassland plains to savanna and woodland, but does not include forested country.

Both an unsuccessful and successful chase leaves its story in the sand to be read by skillful trackers who can judge the age or size of the lion by its spoor. A tracker can discern whether the animal is walking slowly, running or trotting by looking at the patterns formed by the distribution of spoor along the course the animal has taken. A running animal takes longer strides than a walking animal, consequently the distance between the individual pug marks will be greater. The manner in which the sand is kicked up also differs according to the animal's speed and gait, and can readily be interpreted by a good tracker. So too, the progress of a stalk can be explained. The spoor shows where the lion lay frozen for a while – its chest, belly or tail touching the sand – and where it moved forward quickly – the deep scoring print with little kicked-up heaps of sand where the lion took off for the final charge. It shows the gallop of footprints far apart – deep from the heavy landing of the running animal – the distance of the leap onto the prey and signs of the struggle. Bushes and tufts of grass may be unearthed and scattered around the final site of the kill – bloodstains in the sand, still moist if fresh, dried to a dark crust if old. The nearby heap of half-chewed and half-digested plant matter where the prey animal was gutted can be seen, and then the remains of the carcass itself – a head, horns, chewed ribs, broken bones, skin or more.

The San tracker also traces the spoor of the prey back from the killing ground to see how it spent the last few minutes of its life. It may have been resting, unaware of the lions nearby, then suddenly seen or heard the lion in its charge, leapt to its feet, but not quickly enough, as the lion's spoor covering the deeply incised antelope spoor will indicate. The tracker also casts around to see if, in the case of a gemsbok for instance, the victim was part of a herd or whether it was alone, how many companions there may have been, in which direction the others may have run, and whether any of them may have been chased but missed by another member of the lion pride. Evidence of an unsuccessful hunt also remains in the sand. If it was a herd of gemsbok that the lion chased, the San tracker can usually give an account of how many antelope there were, how many were adult or young, and what they were doing. He can determine whether the lion was observed before it charged from too great a distance, and whether the animals got enough of a head start to make a clean escape.

The signs of the taking of small animals are sometimes more difficult to interpret, but the spoor can be read and information gained. In the case of porcupines, quills and pieces of skin are always left behind – as well as other telltale signs, like faeces of the kind that has not yet been voided from the animal. Birds, such as ostriches and an occasional kori bustard, leave feathers behind as testaments. There may also be evidence of the lions finding water and pausing to drink and rest briefly.

All the signs, the spoor and remains are weighed and interpreted by the tracker in telling the story. In addition to acquiring a detailed record of what the lions were stalking, chasing, catching and eating, the distance of each night's travels is measured. The number of rest stops made during the night are recorded, as well as signs of lions having urinated or defecated to mark their territory, and even signs of social interactions among the pride members. From these systematic tracking sessions carried out during the course of regular field trips, an immense body of fascinating information on the Kalahari lion has been amassed.

As illuminating as all the studies undoubtedly are – the better any animal's behaviour and biology is understood, the better its chances of survival will be – there is little that

Right: The common waterbuck of southern Africa has a distinctive whitish ring around the rump.
Opposite: Much of Africa's semi-arid savannas, dominated by small Acacia trees of various species, and shrubs, provides a rich and varied habitat for the great cats and their prey.

can in reality be done in the face of dwindling 'lion country'. The human population continues to grow exponentially and, sadly, as more and more areas are taken for use by livestock at the expense of wildlife, so lion populations will gradually be wiped out. Over most of Africa this process has already taken place – especially in the 50 years since the end of the Second World War. Now very few areas in Africa remain where free-ranging lions are to be found beyond the borders of game parks. In West Africa the lion virtually only survives in protected areas. Some free-ranging lions can be found in the sparsely inhabited parts of East Africa adjoining game reserves, and likewise in the Central African Republic, Zambia, Zimbabwe, Mozambique, Namibia and Botswana. In South Africa, however, lions are today found only in national parks, game reserves and in privately owned wildlife refuges. As long as adequate game populations can be maintained in these areas, the survival of lions can be ensured. A repeat of the great rinderpest epidemic of the 1890s, however, could wipe out game populations over large areas – and with these, the remaining lions.

Africa's rich feline diversity is understandably, yet regrettably, somewhat overshadowed by the relative size and power of the larger members of the family – the lion, leopard and cheetah. Of the smaller cats, the caracal, or African lynx, the serval and the African wild cat are fairly widely known, but few people even know of the existence of the other four members of the group. Secretive, and in some instances severely threatened by habitat degradation and other activities of man, they live much of their lives under cover of darkness, leaving little trace of their passing. Even to scientists many facets of the hidden lives of these carnivores are still to be documented, and little is known other than those basic aspects of biology and behaviour that are common to all cats.

Left: As a killer of livestock the caracal is hunted and persecuted throughout its enormous range, yet it holds its own, and in southern Africa its numbers are increasing.

Right: Out on patrol a caracal is always alert to a chance encounter with potential prey. Its sloping back, caused by the hind legs being longer than the forelegs, is a conspicuous field characteristic.

T he caracal – also referred to as the African lynx – is found from Cape Agulhas at Africa's southern tip to Cape Serte on the shores of the Mediterranean Sea. It is primarily a cat of arid areas, but it occurs in pockets throughout its area of distribution, being absent only from the rainforests and the sandy, arid hearts of the Namib and Sahara deserts.

Beyond Africa the caracal is found sporadically throughout the Arabian Peninsula and the Middle East, and then continues through Iraq, Iran and along the southern shores of the Caspian Sea, where it coexists with the European lynx. Though it is rarely seen, its range also extends across Turkmenia as far north as the edge of the Aral Sea, and then southward through Afghanistan and Pakistan, well into the arid regions of northern and western India.

Throughout Africa, too, caracal numbers have been drastically reduced, except for southern Africa where it is abundant and classified as vermin. Deemed important killers of sheep and goats in some areas, and with a bounty on their heads, these beautiful cats are killed by the thousand each year. While it certainly

is true that some caracal kill stock, it also is true that most do not. They continue to play a vital role in the ecosystem of the arid rangelands of the southern part of Africa, for they and the black-backed jackal are the last, and only, large mammalian predators sharing an often uncomfortable coexistence with man.

This striking medium-sized cat has a stocky, muscular physique with powerful legs, conspicuously large paws, a slender waist and a short tail. The buttocks and hind legs appear disproportionately large and well muscled compared to the forequarters – the hind legs are in fact longer than the forelegs. The caracal's physique gives a clear indication of its hunting style – a stalk, followed by a short rush, lunge or leap at prey which is then grasped by the cat's forepaws. The hindquarters are also adapted to propelling the cat into the air, where it is highly skilled at grabbing birds such as doves, francolin and sand grouse as they rise off the ground.

The caracal's face is sensuous and beautifully marked with contrasting colours which highlight the teeth and blazing eyes when the cat reacts to threat situations. Two black stripes, reminiscent of the cheetah's tear stripes, start on the forehead above each eye, flow along the eye and down on either side of the nose. The caracal's most distinguishing feature, however, consists of its large, sharply pointed and lavishly tufted ears – used as important devices for close range communication with its fellows.

The caracal's specialized habitat requirements are met to perfection in the mountainous terrain of the Eastern Cape Province of South Africa, where its population density is higher than anywhere else. In more open country, such as the savanna habitat in East Africa and Somalia, where caracal are also common, the cats seek out hiding places among rocky outcrops and dense streambank vegetation. Females with kittens are particularly fond of riverine thicket, presumably for protection of their young, and because more rodents, birds and other small game live in such environments. Adult males, and females without young, are less likely to use streambank vegetation. Although not normally forest inhabitants, caracal are also found in the wet, coastal evergreen forest of Knysna along the southern Cape coast.

In the Eastern Cape adult males are more commonly found at higher altitudes on the mountain slopes. Females are inclined to remain in the valleys. This habit may be related to the availability of suitable prey, as large antelope such as mountain reedbuck are generally found at higher altitudes and rodents are abundant in the valleys.

In the Kalahari, where there are no rocks or hills, caracal numbers are low. For lairs and cover the cats utilize dense thickets formed by the shepherd's tree or the low, thorny, spreading thickets of the candle acacia. These colonial growing thickets are formed as young plants spread out and establish themselves in a circle around the original parent plant. The thickets can be as large as 10 metres in circumference, and provide a dense refuge. Smaller animals, including caracal, crawl in underneath the plants' lowest branches, sometimes creating a complex network of paths.

Caracal are largely nocturnal and spend most of the daylight hours lying up in a lair. In remote areas where they are seldom disturbed by humans, they may be abroad during the day. They usually start foraging in the early evening and are active until shortly after sunrise.

Caracal are terrestrial and spend virtually all their time on the ground, but they are adept at climbing trees and jumbled masses of broken rock when necessary. The dens where they rest may be among jumbled boulders beset with dense thicket and grass. Often they choose a site where they can sunbathe on open rock, with a good view of their surroundings, and from where they can bolt into dense cover immediately if disturbed. Their dens are usually well chosen to allow a rapid retreat over dead ground if necessary.

In general, caracal are silent cats, but kittens and subadults communicate by using birdlike chirping sounds, somewhat similar to the calls of cheetah. Like domestic cats, caracal purr when relaxed and growl and spit when angry. A loud coughing call, similar to the leopard's, has also been reported.

They also employ a threat display, usually demonstrated toward other caracal, during which they rise on their toes, with the back arched, tail raised and teeth bared in a snarl. A similar display was described by Professor John Skinner, who watched a caracal in Israel threaten two subadult striped hyaenas at a feeding site.

The caracal, like all cats other than the lion, is essentially a solitary beast. Adults live alone and, where two or more cats are seen together, the group usually consists of a female and her kittens, or a consorting couple. When my wife, Catherina, and I lived for some years in the Mountain Zebra National Park of South Africa, we often saw caracal out hunting at twilight or after dark. Sometimes we found two or three animals together and the size range – always one large adult female and one or two smaller animals – seemed to indicate that the group consisted of a female and her young.

Adult males hold a territory, which they mark, patrol and defend against other adult males. Studies of the movements of radio-collared caracal have shown that, as with leopards, there is a small overlap of range between neighbouring males. In the Eastern Cape mountains the overlap may be as much as 10 per cent of the total range. This overlapping may be due to some extent to the rugged nature of the terrain, but it is not a normal behavioural feature of asocial cats.

Competition for territory between males can be fierce. Radio tracking of marked males has shown how the range of one particular male shrank by half as a more dominant rival moved into an adjoining area and established his territory. The death of an adult caracal leaves a vacuum area for a short while, but in a stable caracal population the opening is soon filled by a new animal – usually a nomadic subadult, leaving its maternal range. The new occupant may not always keep the same boundaries as the predecessor, as neighbours may extend their ranges at the expense of a less-experienced rival. New mutual boundaries and overlap zones are eventually negotiated and established.

Male caracal territories may overlap the ranges of several females. As males' territories are up to three times larger than females' ranges, there are cases where females may have social contact with only one male. In some cases,

The long tufts of hair on the ears of the caracal accentuate their size, shape and position, and probably play an important role – combined with movements of the head – in signalling to other caracal.

111

however, a female's range may fall within the territory of more than one male. Presumably this indicates that she will have more mating opportunities.

Female home ranges also sometimes overlap, but not to the same extent as male territories. In the Eastern Cape the overlap of female ranges has been found to be approximately six per cent of the total range.

Caracal tend to travel along particular paths. The paths also serve as boundaries for territorial males, who leave their mark in the form of scats. The same site often shows signs of old as well as fresh droppings. Presumably this is used to inform other caracal that a cat is in residence. Sometimes caracal also bury their droppings, but they do not regularly restrict themselves to the use of a single latrine or midden as do spotted hyaenas. Little is known about the details of caracal territorial marking, but presumably urine and other chemical secretions serve to convey clear messages to others of their species. Territory holders have been seen urinating on grass tufts, rocks and bushes.

As caracal in the wild are generally dependent upon local or sedentary prey, it is necessary for them to retain near exclusive use of these resources. One can predict, therefore, that territorial marking will be done regularly and, if the chemical warnings are not heeded – especially by wandering subadults – fighting will result. That males regularly meet other males and fight viciously is indicated by the high incidence of scarring and wounding found on the faces of old males.

As males have larger ranges to patrol than females, the average distance travelled by them in a 24-hour period is usually double that of the females. In the Eastern Cape it has been found to be a straight line distance of about four kilometres in males and only about two kilometres for females.

Subadult caracal from the age of about nine months lead a nomadic existence for a time as they begin moving away from the maternal range. Where adjacent ranges are occupied, the young may move as far as 42 kilometres from their birthplace before they can settle and establish their own territory. In South Africa, dispersing subadults who do not know their way around are vulnerable to being hunted by hounds, and so are more easily killed. Elsewhere, where large predators still exist in the wild, young caracal may be killed by leopard or lion.

This wandering phase in the young caracal's life can last for several months. Indications are that subadults try out small ranges for a short period, and, presumably, if they cannot satisfy all their requirements there they move on. This dispersal of subadults is well known to farmers in the Cape – especially those living anywhere near a protected area where caracal are not hunted. As soon as a new cat appears on their land – as evidenced by stock losses – the park or game reserve is labelled as a breeding ground of 'vermin'. The reality, however, is that caracal populations are greater on large farms – albeit at lower densities – than on the few small conserved areas.

The bond, such as it is, between a mating pair of caracal is of short duration. The male detects the onset of oestrus in the female and courting behaviour similar to that of other cats follows. After mating the male carries on with his solitary existence and the female raises her offspring alone.

Kittens – the usual litter size is two – are born in a den or lair lined with hair or feathers, and hidden among rocks in densely thicketed gorges or ravines, in dense bushes on broken ground

Opposite, and this page: The caracal is a specialist at capturing game birds. A careful stalk culminates in a fast rush at birds such as helmeted guinea fowl which immediately take to the air to escape. The powerful hind limbs of the caracal can propel the cat high into the air, however, where it grabs birds with its paws and brings them down.

Below: Like most other cats, the caracal often carries its prey to a convenient place for eating. Opposite: Seasonal rainwater pans in the arid savanna attract not only elephants and other game, but also game birds such as sand grouse.

In the Eastern Cape mountains, on the Karoo plains of the Cape interior and the endless rangelands of southern Namibia, the rock hyrax or dassie is the most abundant mammal above one kilogram. It is estimated that the population of these rabbit-sized colonial herbivores reaches hundreds per square kilometre. The numbers of hyrax are largely determined by habitat factors, particularly the availability of the rocky caves, overhangs and crevices in which they live. They are preyed upon almost exclusively by caracal and the black eagle. Hyrax and caracal seek out the same type of habitat in the Eastern Cape, and it is no surprise that this small herbivore forms the mainstay of the caracal's diet in such areas. As the caracal forages at twilight and at night, and the hyrax is active during the day and sleeps safely hidden under rocks or in crevices at night, the caracal has a limited time in which to take hyrax – mostly just before sunset. During the warm summer months, however, hyrax tend to emerge very early in the morning and remain out foraging late at night. The caracal's method of hunting is highly suited to catching the habitually alert hyrax, as caracal depend upon a quiet, patient stalk and then a quick, short rush to grab their prey.

Caracal are not usually scavengers, and the only reports of their ever taking offal or feeding from carcasses come from Israel, where suitable prey animals may be scarce and caracal are forced to take whatever they can find. It is largely due to the fact that caracal rarely scavenge that they have survived in many parts of Africa, particularly in the sub-Saharan countries of West Africa, where strychnine-poisoned bait has been used over large areas to eliminate scavenging carnivores such as jackal and hyaena.

Like the leopard, the caracal has mastered the art of camouflage and ambush. As opposed to the leopard's ambush, however, the caracal ambush hardly ever originates from a tree. Sometimes it will take up position in a secluded spot close to a game trail among tussocks of tall grass, or under the overhang of leafy bushes and shrubs. There it will patiently lie in wait. In most observed cases, and where the events of the caracal's kill can be interpreted from spoor, it is clear that the prey walked past the caracal without seeing it, and the caracal then attacked its victim from behind. The precaution of attacking from the rear helps the cat evade the prey's defence: a male antelope uses its horns to good advantage when challenged. Duiker, though small, are plucky animals and if they were to face a caracal, the outcome would be highly unpredictable. At least one record exists of a grey duiker male successfully

where concealment is easy, or even down an antbear burrow or in a hole in a tree. The kittens remain hidden in the den while the mother goes out foraging, but as their eyes open and they grow older and stronger, they begin to move around independently. By three to four weeks of age they move around in the den's immediate vicinity and are able to run fairly well.

The kittens stay with their mother until they are fully able to fend for themselves, which is usually at an age of nine to twelve months, although subadults as young as eight months old have been found on their own.

The caracal is an opportunist hunter. It takes a wide range of prey species, within certain clear limits. In general it hunts rodents and larger mammals in the size range of about two to 20 kilograms and birds ranging from doves to game birds like guinea fowl and francolin. Adult males are quite capable of killing prey much larger than themselves such as adult male mountain reedbuck that can reach a weight of more or less 35 kilograms.

Several studies of the caracal's feeding habits have shown that the results vary depending on the nature of the habitat, the range of prey available at the particular time of year or in the particular habitat, and the most abundant species within the size range of caracal prey. In all cases the central conclusions are similar – caracal feed mainly on mammals, but also take birds as a regular and important part of their diet. Occasionally they eat reptiles such as snakes and lizards, and to a lesser extent take invertebrates such as insects and scorpions.

defending itself against a caracal's attack. There is also a record from the southern edge of the Rub' al Khali, the famous 'Empty Quarter' or 'Sand Sea' of the Arabian desert, of a wounded Arabian oryx killing a caracal.

The movements of a stalking caracal, like those of other cats, are tense, deliberate and smooth. The animal moves along as though flattened against the ground, utilizing every scrap of cover. It repeats the action of sliding forward and freezing rapidly – its eyes always on its target, its tail remaining motionless. Usually the final rush is made from a distance of about five metres, when the prey animal is looking away. The caracal's powerful hind legs propel it forward in a flash. It is imperative that it takes the victim by surprise, as most prey can bolt at incredible speed. The large claws on the caracal's forepaws act as hooks

in grabbing fast-moving prey such as hyrax. The caracal then kills the prey with a bite to the throat or neck.

There is still some argument over which bite the caracal favours to achieve a kill. Some observers claim that it is the stranglehold on the throat, similar to that used by larger cats. Others claim that the caracal kills by a powerful bite through the nape of the neck, during which the canines penetrate to the spinal cord or even to the brain case – a technique typical of smaller cats. An adult male caracal's canine teeth are more than 15 millimetres long. In addition, there is a space between the canine and small incisors to the front, and between canine and cheek teeth, which effectively isolate the canines as stabbing spikes which certainly could penetrate to a small victim's spine. In the case of large

Above: A caracal kitten is a fluffy version of the adult, but without such conspicuous ear tufts.
Opposite: The long-crested eagle is characterized by the long, loose, erect feathers on its head.

prey like antelope and sheep, there is a fair thickness of skin and muscle for the teeth to get through before the vital areas of the spine are reached, and in these cases it may be more effective for the caracal to go for the throat.

Once it has killed its prey, the caracal carries or drags it by the neck to the nearest cover, where it begins feeding. Caracal may use a forepaw to swat smaller prey like rats or mice with sufficient force to kill or stun them, then they are picked up in the mouth and carried off to be eaten.

Tame caracal that have been observed hunting, invariably follow a ritual of enfolding the dead prey with the fore- and hind limbs while lying next to it with the jaws firmly clamped on the prey's neck or throat. They then worry at the prey – giving it some quick shakes and pulling it about. This is the same behaviour seen in domestic cats that shake a rat or mouse after killing it. Some observers describe this behaviour as part of the killing process, claiming that the cat can break the spine of its smaller prey by means of this procedure. In the case of the caracal, however, the worrying is usually done after the prey is dead, and the movement is unlikely to damage the spine of an animal the size of a hyrax or larger. The shaking of the prey continues for some minutes, long after the prey is dead. Only when this procedure is complete does the caracal drag the carcass off to a secluded spot and start feeding.

The caracal's jumping ability, to which its powerful hindquarters are so well adapted, really comes to the fore when it is hunting birds. This cat's quick rush at birds feeding on the ground or drinking at a waterhole has often been observed. The caracal takes astonishing leaps and actually rakes birds from the air while keeping its front feet together or by using them singly. There is a sudden blur of cat and feathers as the amazingly agile caracal quite literally flies through the air, using its dewclaw as a hook to impale the rising bird. Jonathan Kingdon reports a caracal leaping to a height of over two metres from a crouched position. A tame caracal raised by Reay Smithers jumped to a measured height of 3.4 metres.

I once witnessed a caracal's fascination with flying prey, and also its ability to catch it. I was returning home from a patrol after dark in the mountains of the Eastern Cape. My Land Rover was bouncing slowly down a rutted, rocky track. Coming around a bend I saw an adult caracal sitting on a rock, blinking in the glare of the vehicle's headlights. I stopped and cut the engine, but left the lights on. After a few moments of staring at the lights, the caracal slowly started walking toward me. Its fixed gaze, alert ears and purposeful movements indicated that it was stalking something. The caracal advanced until it was only a few paces from the car, then it leapt up and grabbed its prey with the sweep of an extended arm. The prey was a small, white moth fluttering toward the car's headlights. I quietly remained there for a while, watching as the caracal caught a few more moths. Then it tired of the game and moved off into the darkness.

An old friend of ours, Ted Reilly, who lives in Swaziland, kept a caracal as a domestic pet. In its old age the cat went blind, but its sense of smell and hearing were so acute that it could still get around the familiar surroundings of the house and garden unaided. One afternoon the caracal was lying on the veranda of the rambling, colonial-style farmhouse where the Reillys lived, seemingly lethargic and dozing. Suddenly, as a small white butterfly came fluttering past, the cat pricked up its ears. With a single leap the blind caracal exploded from the ground, reached out with one paw and cleanly plucked the butterfly from the air.

An intensive study of caracal ecology was carried out in the Mountain Zebra National Park by Lucius Moolman. This park lies in a ruggedly beautiful area in the broken country on the edge of southern Africa's Great Escarpment. This country, with its hills, ridges, perched plateaus and valleys is prime caracal habitat, and presented a wonderful opportunity for research.

To be able to study the movements, population density, extent of home ranges and territories of these elusive cats, it was necessary to fit them with radio collars. The only snag was successfully capturing the cats. Other workers had managed to mark a few caracal at times, but nobody had achieved a major population study, largely because of the difficulties of trapping caracal alive.

Moolman, however, had grown up on a farm in the area and he knew the most likely areas caracal would choose to inhabit. He used large cage traps which were well hidden among bushes next to paths used by caracal. Bait was placed inside the cage and attached to a trigger mechanism. When the cat pulled on the bait, the trap's drop gate was released from its raised position, confining the cat inside.

The following morning the trapper would face the snarling, spitting fury of the caged caracal. Using a pole syringe, the cat was then injected with an immobilizing drug. When the cat was anaesthetized, it could be removed from the trap. It was then examined, weighed, measured and fitted with a radio collar. Even modern immobilizing drugs used on cats are not rapidly reversible, so it is necessary to wait some time before the cat returns to full consciousness. Once the cat is awake and released, the study begins. Some of these marked caracal were located daily for nearly 18 months of continuous tracking.

Over a period of 14 months Moolman caught 21 caracal. His trapping success rate, measured as the number of trap nights on which caracal were caught against the number of trap nights when caracal were not caught, was only one per cent. This figure, low as it is, was nearly five times higher than the success rate achieved by other researchers, clearly indicating the stealth and intelligence of this cat and the difficulty of catching one alive. Moolman calculated that, on average, it took 90 trap nights to ensure one successful capture.

The siting of the trap was found to be a crucial factor in determining the success rate. If the trap was not set close to a path used by the caracal, it would not be caught. The caracal is a creature of habit, using regular paths to patrol its territory, as mentioned before. A caracal could not be induced to move far off its path, even by using aromatic bait such as rotting fish heads. The traps had to be well hidden under piles of brush taken from the immediate vicinity. Branches brought from afar warned the cats off. To enhance the deception, the cage trap's floor was covered with a layer of earth and scattered rocks taken from the area around the trap site. Moolman used various kinds of bait with equal success but discovered that he could make his trap more species-specific by using the urine and droppings of another caracal as the bait to entice the quarry into the cage. By using this bait, which is strongly linked to the caracal's territory patrolling and marking behaviour, other species of animal were deterred from entering these traps.

Moolman's studies enabled him to establish the extent of the home ranges of these cats in different environments, both inside and outside the national park. His work also proved that stock and game fences are no obstacle to the caracal, as it is able to scale them at will.

Many cultures retain signs that the caracal has enjoyed a long history as a domestic pet. The Egyptians, for instance, portrayed these cats in wall paintings and even embalmed their bodies and placed them in tombs. In ancient Persia and the princely states of India, the caracal was trained to hunt small game like hares and birds. A popular Indian sport capitalized on the caracal's ability to take rising birds. Tame caracal were let loose on flocks of pigeons feeding, and bets were then placed on how many birds the cats could ground. Records show that a practised caracal could knock down as many as a dozen pigeons.

Throughout most of southern Africa the caracal is termed a 'problem animal' – an euphemistic phrase used to refer to a stock killer. The caracal lives in open rangeland, in areas where sheep and goats are the prime source of the farmers' income. As these domestic animals fall within the size range of the caracal's natural prey and are easy to kill, they are taken by the cats. In these extensive farming areas the livestock range freely. An obvious precaution to protect the sheep and goats from predation would be to herd them into a stockade or pen at night, but this rarely happens.

Sheep and goats on the range sleep huddled together, making them easy targets, and they are not alert. They are also generally rather unintelligent, and however, that caracal can control hyrax numbers, other than to keep them at their endemic level or natural densities. When predation pressure is removed through eliminating caracal, hyrax colonies experience classic population explosions – their numbers increasing to epidemic proportions. The large numbers of hyrax competing for food with sheep and goats may cost the farmer more in lost production from his rangeland than the episodic losses of stock to caracal. As there may be a natural predator-prey regulatory system – a crash in the hyrax population is quite likely to lead to a decline in caracal numbers – this relationship has been much studied.

Several biologists are currently investigating the influence of caracal and other predators including the African wild cat, black-backed jackal and black eagle on hyrax populations. Supporting the survival of caracal implies both costs and benefits to the farmer. Costs are reckoned in terms of lost lambs and kids. Benefits include reduced hyrax density, thus reduced loss of forage.

The number of caracal killed each year and for which a bounty is paid has been increasing since records were first kept in 1931. It now exceeds a level of 4 000 caracal killed each year in South Africa alone. This situation parallels that found in North America, where the coyote has been increasing steadily and extending its range since it has learnt to live with man.

The increase in caracal numbers can be attributed to various factors. In addition to caracal adapting their habits to their coexistence with humans, they are responding to the effect of human beings eliminating almost all their competitors. Lion, leopard, cheetah and hyaena have almost been wiped out, and the population of black-backed jackal has been reduced drastically.

Left: The crested guinea fowl is the thicket- and forest-dwelling equivalent of the helmeted guinea fowl of the savanna and woodland.
Below: The rock hyrax or dassie is the major prey of the caracal across most of its range in South Africa.

do not flee from predators. In many cases they seem to approach a caracal out of curiosity, the flight instinct having long since been bred out of them. The caracal is then tempted to kill more than one animal, although it can feed off only one. The record kill for two caracal was 22 sheep in one night – all reportedly bitten on the nape of the neck, and showing claw marks on the jowls where the caracal grabbed and held them. When killing domestic stock, however, the caracal is usually selective and takes well-grown lambs or kids. More goats and sheep are killed during the winter months, when hyrax retire to their dens earlier in the evening and emerge only when the sun is well up and caracal are no longer active.

As caracal prey largely on hyrax, which compete for forage with domestic livestock, these cats can be of great use to the landowner. It is not suggested,

THE SERVAL

The serval, unlike the other small cats of Africa, has not been able to retain its historical range which, like that of the larger cats, is declining.

The serval is a medium-sized, long-legged, slenderly built spotted cat with enormous, sensitive ears placed close together on top of a relatively small head. Adult serval have relatively long necks, and can stand as high as 62 centimetres at the shoulder – worthwhile adaptations for a predator which occupies a habitat consisting mostly of tall grass.

The serval is a hunter of the higher rainfall regions of the woodland and savanna zones. It is absent from the drier parts of the African continent such as the Sahara and the region biogeographers refer to as the South West Arid Zone. The latter includes most of Namibia, Botswana and the western half of South Africa, with the exception of the better-watered northern fringes of Namibia and Botswana and the eastern side of South Africa.

Although the range of the serval overlaps to a large extent with that of the similar-sized caracal in high rainfall areas, their habitat preferences and life-styles separate them most effectively. It is also true that while serval populations reach fairly high densities in high rainfall areas, caracal populations do not. Serval are seldom, if ever, found in arid country, in which habitat they are replaced totally by the caracal.

The serval's facial markings and ear colouring are not nearly as dramatic as the caracal's. This probably indicates that the facial patterning does not have the signalling or communication value that is common to the caracal. The ears, in particular, appear to be far more functional hearing appendages, unlike the obvious communication functions displayed by the caracal's strikingly coloured ears with their long, expressive, mobile tufts of black hair.

Among these solitary, predominantly nocturnal hunters, there is no lasting bond between male and female, although pairs may stay together for a while when breeding. Youngsters move around with their mother until they are well grown at the age of nine to twelve months and this accounts for many recorded sightings of 'groups' of serval. Usually there are no more than two young with the adult female. Serval are often seen moving around in the early morning or a few hours after sunrise and are often observed again in the late afternoon, especially during overcast, dull weather. The first serval I ever saw, on the high Nyika Plateau in northern Malawi, was out hunting in grassland on a dull, cloudy afternoon.

Serval are almost entirely terrestrial although they are quite capable of climbing trees if the need arises. The late Reay Smithers, a pioneering mammalogist from Zimbabwe who had a special interest in serval, recorded one serval treed by dogs near Harare. The serval had climbed up the smooth trunk of a tall *Eucalyptus* tree and taken refuge on a horizontal branch about nine metres from the ground. There are many similar records referred to by Lt Col Stevenson-Hamilton, among others. In addition, serval have also been observed climbing trees to take nestlings and roosting birds, or even pursuing a hyrax up a tree.

The serval is a shy, retiring animal and as such, it is rarely seen. It usually hides in reed beds, long grass, or thick scrubby bush areas. It has also been recorded as lying up in antbear burrows or porcupine holes during the day. Sometimes it utters a repetitive, high-pitched plaintive cry – often described by naturalists as 'how-how-how'. The sound is thought to be a form of communication between a serval mother and her kittens, or possibly it is the cat's way of advertising its territory.

When in oestrus, the female serval evidences her condition to neighbouring males by calling and by spraying her urine on conspicuous spots – from which the male presumably scents her condition. Her oestrous call is described by Jonathan Kingdon as a short, sharp miaow which carries far and is repeated in bouts. A receptive female meets an approaching male with purring, and mating is preceded by mutual rubbing.

The serval's gestation period lasts from 68 to 77 days. Records from Zimbabwe indicate that there is a peak in serval births toward the end of the summer months. This peak coincides with the period of the year when rats and mice are most numerous. The rodents' annual population cycle is determined by grasses setting seed at the end of summer, and therefore providing an abundant food supply. At this time of rodent abundance hunting would be easiest for a lactating female serval and this period would, therefore, appear to be the best time for her to be raising kittens.

The newborn kittens are secured in a well-selected, sheltered site in long grass or scrub, in aardvark or porcupine burrows, in hollow logs or amongst rocks. The nursing mother takes great care of her kittens and suckles them for up to six months, though they will take solid food from about three weeks of age. For the first few months the kittens communicate using a birdlike chirping call. The devotion of the mother to her young extends for some months, and there is a case on record of a serval mother steadfastly remaining near a youngster that was caught in a trap – only leaving it when closely approached by humans.

The serval is a specialist hunter of rodents whose chief habitat is long grass, marshland and swampy areas. Mice and rats, and in particular those found in wetter, grass-covered drainage lines are its main prey species. Its physical and behavioural adaptations suit it well for its role as a rodent killer. A serval advances through the grass, slowly and silently, its head held high as it scans the area in front of it for signs of its prey. A serval's highly mobile ears can be cupped and twisted. It moves dead ahead – then a little twist to one side, then the other. Its sight and hearing are excellent and it depends upon these senses for detecting its prey. Observations suggest that serval can pinpoint the slightest sounds made by rats and mice scurrying around in the grass ahead of them. For this reason, perhaps, they are said to be deterred from hunting during windy conditions when the level of background noise or 'clutter' is likely to be high.

The serval's large ears, whilst obviously being used for hunting by sound, possibly have another use – originally suggested by Grif Ewer, a pioneer of carnivore studies. She suggested that the large surface of the ears may well be of some use in dissipating the animal's body heat. Such an explanation may, however, not necessarily be true, as cheetah and leopard – which are larger than serval and live in the same environment – have larger bodies and smaller ears.

Unlike other cats, the serval's hunting technique does not depend upon its stalking animals that are of a size similar to itself. The need for concealment is therefore not as important an element in the hunt. A serval stands at its full height, searching this way and that, before pouncing with a short leap. It kills its prey with a downward blow from a forefoot, delivered with great force. It may also jump high in the air and then strike the prey with all four feet on landing before biting it. This leaping jump may even be repeated several times in a stotting action like that of a springbok, creating the impression of the serval bouncing through the grass. If the prey is seen from a distance it may be stalked in a typically feline way with the serval crouching low on the ground and then making a short rush to catch the prey. Our colleague, Petri Viljoen, who studied lions in the Savuti area of Botswana, once observed a serval hunt and kill a springhare. The serval was moving through a stand of tall grass, the

Opposite, and above: Mice and rats are the main prey species taken by serval, who adopt a typically upright posture with ears cocked and pointing forward to locate sounds of movement in the grass.

Left: The enormous ears of the serval indicate the importance of hearing to this hunter.
Opposite, above: The grey crowned crane is a bird of the better-watered southeastern part of Africa, where it shares its range in moister grasslands and drainage lines with serval.
Opposite, below: The scrub hare is widespread in Africa and at times forms part of the diet of most of the cats.

nearest springhare less than two metres away. A swift approach by the cat was followed by a leap. The springhare was caught by the throat and suffocated. It was then carried off, the serval holding it by the neck.

Serval are noted for using their paws, rather than their teeth, to catch rats and mice. Often rodents are hooked and tossed up in the air before being pounced upon and bitten. The claws on the serval's front feet are particularly sharp and strongly curved, thus forming efficient hooks for grabbing prey. Serval have also been seen digging small prey out of crevices and holes, and mole rats out of their underground runs. The serval's dewclaws are well developed, but the claws on its hind feet are shorter and seldom used.

Serval often play with their prey after killing it, tossing the body up into the air with a quick movement of the head, and then either standing upright on their hind legs to swipe the prey as it falls, or pouncing on it when it hits the ground. Jonathan Kingdon records how this prey-tossing action can, when a bird is the prey, change imperceptibly into a feather-plucking action.

The main source of information on the serval's feeding habits in southern Africa is derived from an analysis of the stomach contents of 65 serval collected during research being done in Zimbabwe. This analysis shows that rats and mice are by far the most important food source, as measured both by the percentage of occurrence of these groups in the sample and the variety of species eaten. There were 12 species of rats, mice or gerbils recorded in the Zimbabwe samples, an insectivorous shrew, a scrub hare, various birds and snakes, a lizard, a chameleon, a frog and various insects.

The most abundant rodents taken were the multimammate mouse and the Angoni vlei rat. The mouse is the most common small mammal species found in the Harare area, and it also is found in a wide range of habitat types throughout sub-Saharan Africa, but is absent from the South West Arid Zone. Multimammate mice are a species commonly commensal with humans, and are widespread in villages and homes. Their numbers can fluctuate widely and they can, given the right conditions, erupt in hordes in a short period of time. The multimammate mouse can have up to twelve pairs of nipples, and can therefore produce and feed a large number of young. These mice are also less secretive than most other rodents and are predominantly nocturnal, being most active just after sundown and before sunrise. The latter factors, together with their abundance, probably ensures the species a high ranking in the diet of rodent-eaters like owls and serval. As multimammate mice are an important host of diseases like plague and other viruses which affect humans, the serval is potentially useful to humans every time it eats one.

The Angoni vlei rat is not nearly as abundant, nor as readily available, as the multimammate mouse. Its habitat requirements, however, exactly match the ideal habitat of the serval. Angoni vlei rats are found from South Africa to Kenya, but only in higher rainfall areas in marsh, vlei, swamp, drainage line and streambank habitats. Angoni vlei rats are predominantly diurnal, but can be active at night. Presumably their activities during the late afternoon and early morning overlap sufficiently with the time of the activities of the nocturnal serval, as they feature prominently in the serval's diet. The fact that Angoni vlei rats are also reportedly eaten by owls indicates some nocturnal or at least crepuscular activity.

The overlap of habits and habitats between the serval and the nocturnal marsh, reed-bed and drainage-line grassland rodents is, of course, no accident. It clearly indicates the serval's high degree of specialization in exploiting a particular niche in which there are no other significant mammalian predators. The mosaic nature of African habitats also helps to explain the overlap of range between serval and caracal – although they may occur in the same general area, they exploit very different habitats and prey reservoirs.

Serval also often take birds. Although they have been recorded taking guinea fowl, quail, spurfowl and bustards on occasion, they mostly take small birds. Among those that have been recorded in their diet are red-billed quelea, waxbills, weavers, bishops and widow birds – all of which roost in reed beds or clumps of long grass in damp areas. The serval is not in the same class as the caracal when it comes to catching birds on the wing, but it does have a prodigious leaping ability which it utilizes to spring on the bird, grab it with its claws and then dispatch it with a quick bite to the neck. Serval can also stretch upright to take birds and, if given the opportunity, can quite easily become killers of domestic fowl. Such poultry raiders have been known to return to the same run or even to a carcass, where they can be trapped. They have not been observed taking other carrion, however.

Smaller food items found in the serval's diet include insects and snakes and the lesser musk shrew, a small insectivore, which pays the price of sharing the serval's habitat. It is a common although unimportant component of the serval's diet, but interesting nonetheless, as it is seldom found in the diets of any of the other cats.

The serval is tolerant of human beings and resilient in the face of development. As it can live for up to twenty years, it presumably can adapt in the face of changing circumstances in its range which it shares with man. It is likely that this cat's range has not changed as markedly as that of others of the group, which are less compatible with human beings and their livestock. The serval has been eliminated from its former range along the southern Cape coast and the Cape Peninsula, however.

Whereas caracal regularly kill livestock, there are no definite records of serval taking domestic stock, although individuals occasionally do take poultry. As human settlements often result in increased rodent populations, the serval may be more abundant in some areas than was the case a few decades ago. At night serval may sometimes be found hunting quite close to human dwellings.

THE BLACK-FOOTED CAT

Smallest of the African cats, the diminutive black-footed cat is endemic to the arid regions of southern Africa.

The black-footed cat is one of the smallest of the world's 34 cat species. It is also the rarest cat in southern Africa. As it is so rarely encountered, very little is known of its behaviour and biology. It is widely, but sparsely, distributed through the lower rainfall areas of South Africa, Botswana and Namibia.

In recent years there has been a regrettable attempt on the part of some zoologists to change the common name of the black-footed cat to 'small spotted cat'. It is argued that the African wild cat also occasionally has black feet and that the two species are, therefore, easily confused. How any observant person can confuse a spotted cat like the black-footed cat with the completely unspotted African wild cat, is difficult to understand, however.

The name 'black-footed cat' has been used since the nineteenth century, and it is not clear how anything can be gained by changing it now. Within South Africa, the name 'small spotted cat' will undoubtedly cause confusion with the 'small-spotted genet', which, although a member of the mongoose family, is often regarded as a cat by laymen. Furthermore, the proposed name 'small spotted cat' is also likely to cause international confusion with the 'little spotted cat', an accepted alternative common name of the oncilla *Leopardus tigrinus* which is found from Costa Rica to Argentina.

As in the case of the other small and elusive cats, very little information on the black-footed cat is available, and its behaviour and ecology in the wild have never been comprehensively studied. What we do know of this secretive little cat is based largely on chance observations of live animals in the wild, on the limited data derived from collected animals, and on those that have been successfully kept in captivity, and one recent field study.

The black-footed cat is a solitary animal. With few exceptions, sightings in the wild have been made at night. During the day the cat hides in antbear, springhare or porcupine burrows, caves, dense tangles of low thicket and other secluded spots. It usually emerges several hours after sunset and, in areas where it is likely to be disturbed, it is not active at all at dusk. In the remote Kalahari Gemsbok National Park it has occasionally been reported to move around at dawn and dusk. In captivity, where artificial feeding regimes regulate the cats' lives, they are active during the day. They have been reported to show either strong mate attachments in captivity or a high degree of intolerance toward other members of the species.

Most texts describe the black-footed cat as being ferocious and intractable. This little cat is reported to be more antisocial in captivity than any other cat species. Paul Leyhausen and Barbara Tonkin speculated that the fierceness of this cat, its antisocial behaviour, and the short time spent on mating behaviour, may be linked to its ecological status. Being a small, relatively defenceless, secretive cat living in open country, constant alertness and vigilance are essential. This little cat cannot allow social behaviour to reduce its watchfulness and consequently expose it to danger. There may be some truth in this reasoning, and the general picture is certainly supported by the secretiveness and readiness to flee and hide, which are characteristics of this beautiful little cat. Its enemies are most likely to be other carnivores and possibly eagle owls.

The specimen which Paul and I saw together – the first one that I had ever seen in the wild – was an adult. We were driving slowly through the bush at night, shining a spotlight from side to side as we moved along, looking for the telltale glow of eyes in the beam of light. The black-footed cat's eyes showed up brilliantly. When we spotted it, the cat immediately froze and sank down onto its belly behind a small bush. It watched us as we approached it cautiously, and then it suddenly turned and hurried away, darting from cover to cover as it fled. Since then I have seen several black-footed cats at Addo Elephant National Park in the Eastern Cape Province of South Africa – always solitary adults moving about late at night. Visitors to Addo, going out on the very popular night drives conducted by a field guide or ranger, also occasionally see black-footed cats. This is one of very few areas where tourists stand a chance of seeing the rarest cat in southern Africa.

Many published pictures show a caged black-footed cat, snarling and spitting at the camera, its ears completely flattened like wings attached to the sides of its head, the black gape of the mouth highlighted by a bright pink tongue, showing off the sharp white canines. A recent article by Walter Mangold takes strong issue against this stereotyping of the black-footed cat. In his well-illustrated article in *African Wildlife*, Mangold argues that he has kept several black-footed cats at a sanctuary near Cape Town and that, if treated with care and kindness, they tame down completely and are no more vicious than the average household kitten. Dr Paul Leyhausen also reported a captive male that was quite trusting, but a female that remained very shy of human contact.

Captive black-footed cats have been reported to spray urinate on conspicuous points in their surroundings. We can, therefore, reasonably conclude that, like other cats, they have a strong territorial system leading them to mark out territories with scent, and defend territories against conspecifics. There must be considerable overlap between the ranges or territories of males and females. As these cats are rare and live at low densities, it is fair to assume that their ranges are large. The observed habit of these cats in captivity to trot around for hours on end seems to indicate that they may cover relatively long distances every night in the wild.

The black-footed cat is reported to have a short oestrous period, lasting for as little as a few hours to no more than two days. The actual period when the female is prepared to accept the male lasts for only from five to ten hours, and no more than half a dozen copulations occur during this time. This brevity of the oestrous period is in strong contrast to other small cats, in which mating takes place for at least three to four days and the full oestrous period lasts for about six days. As mentioned previously, Leyhausen and Tonkin argue that this may be part of the black-footed cat's lifestyle in order to minimize the amount of time that mating cats may be vulnerable to predation. One may further conclude that, as it is a solitary species, the male black-footed cat is able to detect the onset of oestrus in the female in good time to ensure successful mating. Courtship most likely takes place as with other cats, although presumably for a briefer period. After mating the male and female part company.

The gestation period is about 68 days and a litter of one to three kittens is born in a burrow or some other hiding place. Although kittens of captives have been described, no newborn kittens in the wild have yet been described.

Droughts, or at least unreliable rainfall, are a feature of the arid regions occupied by this cat and this can result in dramatic fluctuations in rodent populations, and, therefore, of the black-footed cat's main food supply. It would not be surprising to find that in years where rodent numbers are low, the cats may not be as successful at raising young.

Although no observations of the behaviour of kittens in the wild are known, there is some information on captives in European zoos and, more recently, at the Animal Rehabilitation Centre near Pretoria, which is run by Karen Trendler. An intriguing aspect of this information is that the kittens, when disturbed, do not run back to the den to hide. Instead, they scatter to the nearest cover and then freeze until the mother gives an audible all-clear signal. Leyhausen and Tonkin describe this call as a staccato 'ah-ah-ah' sound which

Most opportunities for studying the behaviour of black-footed cats have been presented by those in captivity, and scientists have shown avid interest.

black-footed cats taken during a mammal survey of Botswana. His samples showed various rodents, spiders, reptiles, insects and birds.

Nothing is known of the black-footed cat's hunting technique, but it probably stalks and pounces on its prey like domestic cats. It kills rodents with the neck bite, the long canine teeth severing the spinal column. This method of killing is typical of small cats. The two foundling Karoo kittens were kept in captivity in the Karoo National Park until they were adult. As part of the preparation for their release they were fed live prey in their enclosure, including birds such as familiar chats. They readily caught the birds by jumping up at them and hooking them with a paw, before taking the bird to the ground and delivering the killing bite to the neck.

The black-footed cat is rare, but there is no indication that it is in any imminent danger of extinction, or that any major change in its distribution or status is likely. Due to the fact that it is too small to tackle domestic livestock, it is not regarded as a problem animal. It is so secretive and retiring that it is seldom trapped or killed during the course of the hunting of stock-raiding species like caracal and black-backed jackal. It appears always to have been rare wherever it has occurred, and, as long ago as 1934, Shortridge reported that an avid collector of black-footed cat skins on the border between Namibia and Botswana could gather only 15 skins over a period of 12 years.

In 1934 Shortridge was the first scientist to comment on hybrids or crosses between black-footed cats and domestic cats. Hybrids have also been produced in captivity from the mating of a male black-footed cat with a female domestic cat. The resulting crosses were not fertile, however.

Black-footed cats have for years been kept in captivity with African wild cats with no interbreeding reported. This would seem to be borne out by the fact that the two species occur sympatrically in the wild – the African wild cat occurring wherever the black-footed cat is found – with no natural hybrids having ever been reported. There is no other evidence of hybridization occurring in the wild and so far it does not appear as though genetic dilution is as much of a threat to this species as it undoubtedly is to the African wild cat.

is accompanied by synchronous up-and-down movements of the mother's half-flattened ears. On hearing this sound, the kittens relax and leave their cover to gather around the mother. Two kittens picked up in the middle of a road near the Karoo National Park may well have been obeying the instinct to freeze when found. Another intriguing possibility is that the mother may have been in the process of moving the kittens when she was disturbed by the approaching vehicle and fled, leaving the kittens behind.

When the kittens are about five weeks old the mother starts bringing live prey to them, releasing it in front of the kittens and then allowing the youngsters to catch and kill it. If the prey looks as though it might escape, she drives it toward the kittens again. In this way the kittens learn to capture, kill and manipulate their prey.

Captive black-footed cats are still immature at the age of 15 months, and sexual maturity has been reported at 21 months, which is somewhat later than these developments in other small cats.

Considering its size and strength one can correctly conclude that the black-footed cat is a hunter of small prey. The best information available on the diet of the black-footed cat was published by Reay Smithers, a pioneer African naturalist and mammal taxonomist. He recorded the stomach contents of seven

THE AFRICAN WILD CAT

In shape, form and behaviour the African wild cat is sufficiently similar to the familiar domestic cat as to leave little doubt that it represents the ancestral form.

The African wild cat is one of the most ubiquitous of the savanna cats – always seeming to be present everywhere. Records show that it was probably already domesticated by the ancient Egyptians at least 5 000 years ago. The domestic cats of Europe are regarded as being almost certainly descended from the African wild cat *Felis silvestris lybica,* and not from the closely related European wild cat *Felis silvestris silvestris.*

The African wild cat occurs right across the continent, being absent only from the extreme deserts and evergreen forests. It does, however, occur widely along the edge of the main forest blocks in Zaïre, Angola and the Central African Republic, and is able to survive in the mosaic of forest patches and tall woodland which is the typical vegetation of the transition zone from the forest to woodland and savanna.

This cat gives the overriding impression of being lithe and long-legged, with speckled grey fur, against which black bands on the legs and tail stand out

prominently. In most parts of Africa there has been, in modern times, considerable inbreeding between African wild cats and domestic cats, and purebred wild cats are now only to be found in the remotest areas.

The long, slender legs are conspicuous, and these, together with high shoulder blades, give the African wild cat the look of a cheetah, rather than that of a slinking leopard. The long front legs also raise the body into a near vertical position when the African wild cat sits upright – this posture being impossible for the domestic cat or the shorter-legged European wild cat.

The African wild cat is tolerant of a wide range of habitats, occurring from sea level to 3 000 metres in mountains, and from arid semi-desert to well-watered woodlands. It avoids open country, as it requires cover for lying up and hunting. It finds cover around rocky hillsides, termite-mound thickets, shrubs, reed beds, long grass, riverine scrub or thicket and wooded kloofs or ravines.

In the Kalahari – which is mostly a grass-covered semi-desert – these cats use clumps of close-growing *Acacia* bushes, or the denser vegetation of the

Left: The grooming habits of an African wild cat include using the hind foot to scratch the body vigorously. This probably removes ectoparasites, dirt and knotted fur.
Opposite: Characteristic of the African wild cat are its long front legs which allow it to sit in a more upright position than the domestic cat.

Territories are clearly marked out by spraying urine on prominent places and by scratching on trees. Territorial combat is fierce and is usually accompanied by much yowling, growling and spitting.

African wild cats are mostly nocturnal and are rarely seen abroad during either daylight or twilight. They usually spend their days resting in a sheltered spot, for example in dense bushes, up a tree, down an antbear burrow or among rocks and brush, and only move around after dark. In remote areas like the Kalahari, they may occasionally be seen during the day. They are secretive and cunning and move around with care and great stealth. Usually they move a short distance, then stop and sit, taking careful stock of their surroundings before moving on. This probably helps them to avoid the larger predators which often kill them, and also helps them to detect prey at a distance.

If taken from the wild before their eyes have opened, African wild cats tame easily. They quickly adapt to a domestic environment, but may also wander off into the wild for varying periods of time, returning when it suits them. Reay Smithers kept two females as pets and he described how demanding of affection and attention the cats were, especially after returning from one of their 'walkabouts'. They would purr loudly, stretch and rub themselves against his legs to elicit a response. He also described them as being inveterate thieves, jumping up onto the table at meal times to scrounge food. When threatened the cats would draw back their ears, bare their fangs, spit and strike out. Strange dogs would elicit the typical arched-back defensive cat posture.

African wild cats habitually bury their faeces. In part this may be a mechanism to avoid attracting the attention of larger carnivores, most of which will kill the cats if they can catch them, but it may also constitute part of the territory-marking behaviour. The ritual is performed in a very deliberate way with the cat first scratching a depression in the ground with the front feet,

inter-dune valleys and seasonal watercourses for cover. On the arid gravel plains of Namibia they use the sparse woody plant growth of watercourses and rocky gorges as their lying-up areas and hunting grounds. Similar habitat is occupied on the Ahaggar Plateau in Algeria and on the Arabian Peninsula. African wild cats have also been recorded using the burrows of other animals, such as aardvark and fennec in Africa and red foxes in Oman, and the exposed roots of fallen trees for cover.

The African wild cat is the quintessential feline – nocturnal, solitary, independent, wary and aloof. It is mostly terrestrial, but can climb well – quickly taking to trees when hunting, if cornered, or even just to find a convenient resting site. The habit of running for a tree when pursued has been recorded from localities as far afield as Botswana and Oman. Each cat occupies its own territory and it is likely that the territory of a male overlaps or adjoins that of several females. Individuals defend their territories against trespassers of either sex, unless it is a meeting between a male and a female in oestrus.

Left: Safety in numbers – this is how a flock of ground-dwelling birds like helmeted guinea fowl protect their young from predators such as African wild cats.
Right: Interbreeding with the domestic cat poses the greatest threat to the long-term survival of the African wild cat.

dropping the scats and then covering them by scraping the ground, again using the front feet. Sometimes the cats use the same site regularly, establishing small latrines where the scats accumulate.

When disturbed, the African wild cat will crouch down, first watching the source of the disturbance, and then moving off at a quick trot in a crouched position. It usually moves in bursts over short distances, frequently looking back over a shoulder at the cause of the disturbance.

African wild cats follow the hunting technique typical of cats, which involves a careful stalk to get as close as possible to potential prey. The cat then crouches down, eyes fixed on the quarry, settling its hind feet under its body to ensure a good grip on the ground. At the right moment it launches itself into a fast rush at the prey. The cat grabs its prey using its front feet with the claws extended, and delivers the killing bite to the back of the neck in the case of small mammalian prey or birds.

When dealing with larger prey such as hares, the wild cat may grab the prey, throw itself on its side, and then rake the prey animal with its hind claws while using the neck bite to hold on to it. This position is somewhat reminiscent of the position adopted by the caracal, which lies and enfolds its prey with its paws while maintaining its grip on the throat.

The African wild cat is predominantly a hunter of small rodents, birds, small reptiles and insects. It also takes other invertebrates such as hunting spiders, scorpions and centipedes. Occasionally it eats fruit. The food types utilized by this cat evidences a fairly uniform variety over the extensive range of the species. This has been demonstrated by analyzing and comparing the stomach contents taken from cats collected in Botswana, Zimbabwe and Oman. The African wild cat has not been recorded as taking carrion of any kind.

When she is in oestrus, the female African wild cat may attract several males to her territory. It may be presumed, therefore, that there is some element of competition for her favours amongst the available males. It has even been suggested by some researchers that the presence of more than one male may be necessary to stimulate the female to mate. Apparently mating in the wild has not been witnessed, or if it has, it has not been well documented, as none of the standard texts on African mammals make any reference to it. Mating presumably takes place in much the same way as in the domestic cat, with the courting male making his intentions known by much noisy yowling. The female is in oestrus for two to three days and, if not mated, she returns to oestrus every six weeks. The gestation period is approximately 60 days, with records ranging from 56 to 65 days.

The average litter size is three, but it can range from two to five kittens, and occasionally consists of only one. The kittens are generally born in a sheltered lair of some kind – in a hollow tree, among crevices in rocks, in dense thickets, stands of tall grass, or quite commonly in holes in the ground originally excavated by aardvark or springhare. In the Arabian Peninsula fox earths are sometimes used. The mother does not usually collect bedding material, although leaf litter will be used if it is available. In southern Africa most of the young are born during the summer months, but closer to the equator kittens are born almost all year round.

Free-ranging tame African wild cats have produced as many as three litters in the course of a year. In southern Africa it is unlikely, however, that they would ever produce more than one litter a year in the wild, although two litters are possible. The kittens grow quickly and reach half their adult size in about three months. At about this age they start accompanying their mother and learn hunting techniques. At four to five months of age the youngsters can hunt for themselves, and they begin to be independent.

The African wild cat's world is a dangerous one. Among its enemies are caracal, leopard, lion, pythons and dogs – occasionally it may also be killed by birds of prey. I once came across a devastating scene in the Timbavati area of

Mpumalanga in South Africa where a tawny eagle had killed an adult African wild cat and was busy eating it. Judging by the spoor, clawed-up ground, feathers and fur scattered around, the cat had put up a spirited defence. The eagle had crushed the cat's spine in its talons, and had used its sharp beak to pull out the entrails. The carcass of the cat was still fresh when I came upon the scene at midday and so I assumed that the wild cat had, uncharacteristically, been abroad during daylight. The eagle is a strictly diurnal raptor and it must have come upon its unusual prey by chance. The remains of an African wild cat have also been found in the nest of a bateleur eagle, but this cat may have been killed by some other animal and picked up by the eagle as carrion.

Wherever African wild cats and domestic cats come into contact with one another, interbreeding between the two species occurs. The progeny are fertile and therefore, in many areas, it is now becoming increasingly difficult to find purebred African wild cats. This was clearly illustrated to me when I photographed a grey and white hybrid cat in Botswana, in the dry bed of the Nossob River in the Kalahari, about 30 kilometres from the nearest settlements. To avoid further contamination of the gene pool of the African wild cat, several African countries have now made it standard practice to ban the keeping of domestic cats by staff living in national parks.

Many hybrids are very much like wild cats in appearance, but there are two distinctive features of the African wild cat which the hybrids do not have. The first is the rich reddish colour of the back of the ears, and the second is the African wild cat's unusually long legs.

There are records of hybrid matings between African wild cats and serval from Zimbabwe, as described by Reay Smithers. Several litters were known and a number of the hybrids grew to maturity. They had the general build of a wild cat, but with shorter legs, and had the markings of a serval. These hybrids did not appear to be fertile.

Many small antelope, like the red-flanked duiker, are well able to defend themselves against the smaller predators like the African wild cat. Their young are vulnerable for a short period.

THE SWAMP CAT

Right: The shortish, banded tail and large ears are features of the swamp cat which, in Africa, is confined to the lower Nile valley.
Opposite: The swamp cat, like the serval to which it is thought to be closely related, occupies marsh and grassland habitat, where it excels as a hunter of rodents.

The swamp cat is essentially a denizen of Asia, where it is more commonly known as the 'jungle cat'. In Africa the cat's range is marginal, and the niche it occupies in Asia is largely occupied in Africa by the serval, a cat of similar size and habits.

The range of the swamp cat in Africa is small compared with the extensive range of the species in Asia. There are records of swamp cats along the Nile, from the delta along the Nile valley for about 90 kilometres south of Cairo and west of the river. The range of the swamp cat then continues farther south for about 350 kilometres. There is also a record from Mersa Matruh, about 240 kilometres west of Alexandria. Haltenorth and Diller mention the occurrence of this cat in the Ahaggar and Tassili N'Ajjer mountains in southern Algeria. The presence of the swamp cat in the latter localities seems rather improbable, as these are isolated mountainous areas which lie in the middle of the Sahara. There is little, if any, suitable habitat there other than in small, isolated, relict patches of vegetation above 1 800 metres.

In Africa and the Middle East the habitats preferred by the swamp cat are usually described as being swampy or moist areas with tall grass and reed beds, or thickets in the vicinity of water. The swamp cat coexists well with humans, and is quite at home in cultivated fields and in gardens on the outskirts of villages. As the Nile valley and major river valleys of the Middle East are intensively settled and cultivated, the swamp cat has little choice but to share its habitat with humans, or else disappear.

The swamp cat is of medium size with body proportions ranging between those of the African wild cat and caracal, but with the long-legged, rangy build of the serval. The most striking features of the swamp cat are its large pointed ears – the backs having a conspicuous rusty tinge, and the fronts being buffy-white. The ears are set on a fairly large head. The tips of the ears carry short tufts of black hair – not quite as long as the tassles of the caracal, but more conspicuous than those of any of the other smaller cats.

Swamp cats are retiring, secretive creatures and although mainly nocturnal in habit, they are often seen out hunting during the day. They take a wide range of prey items – from snakes, lizards, frogs and fish to birds, rodents and even medium-sized mammals.

There is little available literature concerning the swamp cat's hunting technique. It is, however, a fast-moving, agile creature and one can speculate on its watching, stalking and pouncing on its prey. It is known to be a good

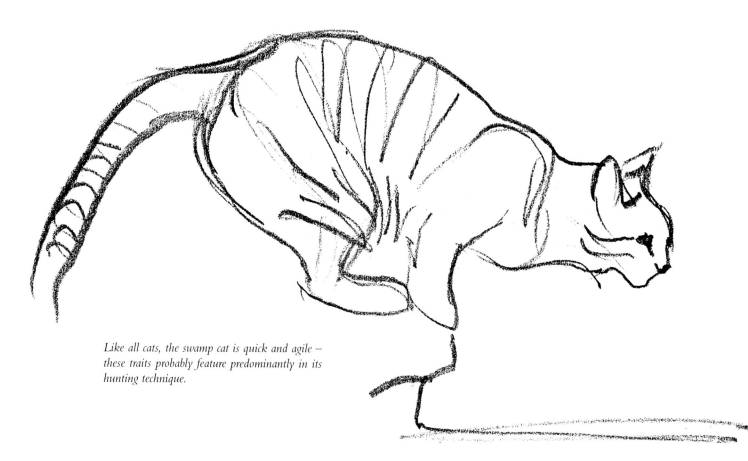

Like all cats, the swamp cat is quick and agile – these traits probably feature predominantly in its hunting technique.

climber of trees. It can also run fast, as can most cats, and has been recorded running at approximately 30 kilometres per hour along a road in front of a vehicle before it accelerated to a much higher speed. The swamp cat has no aversion to water and swims well.

E P Gee reports a swamp cat scavenging from the remains of two bullocks that had been killed by Asiatic lions in India's Gir forest. This seems to indicate a degree of opportunism on the part of this cat. Whether scavenging is a habit of swamp cats elsewhere is not recorded. Gee's report is equally telling of the relationship between the swamp cat and birds, in this case vultures. These birds were less concerned at the presence of six lions at the kill than of a single swamp cat, at whose appearance they fled.

A swamp cat will lie up in a den among rank vegetation or in the vacant burrow of another animal. The den is well prepared and well hidden – one in which kittens were in found in Azerbaijan was described as 'a reed den on the ground beneath a bush'. The mother takes great care of her kittens, feeding, grooming and defending them. The offspring are independent at about five months of age and sexually mature at approximately 18 months.

Little is known about the swamp cat's social behaviour. It seems that these cats are solitary animals that occupy a fairly well-defined territory which they presumably defend against others of their own kind. Males and females meet for mating and then go their separate ways, although family groups have occasionally been seen in the wild. The swamp cat makes a harsh mewing call which is used to facilitate contact between male and female.

The raising of the kittens is done by the mother alone. While mating between the smaller varieties of cats is usually an affair between only two animals (or sometimes with a second, unsuccessful suitor also being attracted to the vicinity), domestic cats occasionally congregate socially at a meeting place which is usually adjacent to, or on the fringes of, a particular territory. Such congregations may involve several individuals, adults and subadults, and undoubtedly play some role in the social arrangements of the cats. George Schaller referred to the observation of such a congregation of swamp cats in Kanha National Park in central India. He related this gathering of several swamp cats to mating behaviour.

Similar social congregations have also been observed in lynx and tiger populations, but this behaviour is not necessarily linked to mating, and the true function of such gatherings is as yet unknown.

THE SAND CAT

The sand cat is regarded as a northern relative of the black-footed cat. These two small cats share many similarities of size, behaviour and lifestyle.

The sand cat is a rare and specialized desert dweller found in a few isolated localities dotted across a vast range of desert country from the Sahara to Pakistan. As this cat inhabits the remotest and most inhospitable parts of this habitat, it has seldom been seen. Very few specimens are known to science and little is known about its behaviour or ecology. It has never been intensively studied in Africa, though recent field studies in Israel and work on captives have yielded much information.

The most striking features of the sand cat are its very large ears and the hairy undersides of its feet. The triangular ears are set far apart on a large, square-looking flat-topped head. The ears are very broad at the base, extending down the side of the cat's face, and have a pointed apex.

Sand cats have been kept in captivity, but very little has been published about them to date. They are reported to be fierce and intractable. A sand cat from Beihan in southern Yemen lived in the London Zoo for seven-and-a-half years and Rosevear reported that it had a 'constant surly look'. The cat flattened its ears and spat at anyone attempting to handle it. Eventually, however, it did allow handlers to scratch its head, but it would never voluntarily approach anyone for this purpose as a domestic cat does.

In effect the sand cat must be far more abundant than the dearth of records and observations would seem to indicate, as viable populations seem to exist over very large areas, and the longevity of this species is unlikely to be greater than 12 to 15 years.

The sand cat is probably similar in most respects to other small cats. It lives a solitary life, is largely nocturnal, and in Africa it preys on small animals such as gerbils, squirrels, snakes, lizards, small birds and insects. Specimens found in Asia reportedly prey on desert rodents. As there is no permanent water in the range occupied by sand cats, it is possible that they never drink, securing sufficient moisture from their food instead. Like other desert-adapted animals, they probably have very efficient kidneys and possibly also produce very concentrated urine. The sand cat is active after dark and is known to wander far over a large home range – presumably in search of widely scattered food sources and a possible mate.

The sand cat lives in shallow burrows in the sand or among the roots of desert bushes. In Turkmenistan – now an independent state, but once part of the USSR – tucked in behind Turkey and Iran, their burrows are reported as being among the roots of saltbushes and calligonum plants (plants of the

While the sand cat is extremely rare because of the limitations of its specialized habitat, there is no reason to believe that it is endangered.

genus *Calligonum* are also found in the sandy areas of the Sahara). One African specimen was observed entering a hole in a sand dune from which it was subsequently excavated by researchers. Living underground is an obvious adaptation to avoid the extremes of the desert climate.

Virtually nothing is known about the reproduction of sand cats other than the much-quoted 1935 report by Ognev, based on his observation of sand cats from Turkmenia, and for half a century this was virtually the only information available. Based on recent work on sand cats in captivity, the average litter size seems to be about three. Studies suggest that sand cats are similar in most aspects of their biology to the black-footed cat and the African wild cat.

The sand cat illustrates a combination of several anatomical and behavioural features which help it survive in its desert environment. Among its physical adaptations are its pallid colouring, hairy feet, large ears and enlarged tympanic bullae (bony projections in the middle ear). These features are also found in other groups of mammals adapted to desert life. There are several parallels to the hairy feet of the sand cat to be found in Arabian mammals, such as the three-toed jerboa and the Arabian hare. Both these mammals also have very hairy feet that assist them in moving across sand. The desert race of the red fox in southern Arabia also has hairy feet, while other races of the same species found further to the north do not.

Another interesting feature of desert animals is their enlarged ears. A few examples of this feature found in the same environment as the sand cat in Africa and Arabia are the fennec fox, Ruppell's sand fox and the two species of desert hedgehogs, the long-eared hedgehog and the Ethiopian hedgehog, all of which have much larger ears than their relatives from moister climates, as do the three-toed and long-eared jerboas and the desert dormouse of Arabia. Even the Arabian hare, a member of a group characterized by large ears, shows relatively larger ears than related hares which do not live in desert environments.

The enlarged ears of desert animals, which may contribute to greater auditory acuity, also play a role in thermoregulation. The large surface area of the ears, with superficial blood circulation, assists in dissipating heat from the body. Conversely, arctic mammals tend to have reduced ear size to minimize heat loss. Zoologists refer to this principle as Allen's rule.

The enlarged tympanic bullae of desert animals is also found in many mammalian groups. It has been experimentally shown that the enlarged bullae result in better hearing than animals with smaller bullae. The more acute hearing can help predators (such as the sand cat) to detect moving prey, and in the case of the prey (such as gerbils) to possibly avoid predation. In solitary desert species which live at very low population densities the more acute hearing may assist in locating mates for reproduction. In the case of *Meriones crassus*, a gerbil or jird which is widespread in the Sahara and Arabia, but which has a low population density, the range of most acute hearing is concentrated around the same frequency as the feeble call that they make. This clearly suggests that at least in these gerbils, their enlarged tympanic bullae confer a greater ability to hear the cry of others of their kind. This is likely to be beneficial to a species living in dispersed populations. If it could be shown that there is a similar relationship between the hearing and calling frequencies of the sand cat, then a similar conclusion relating to social contact could be made. It is known that the sand cat makes a loud mewing contact call, so this may be a valid suggestion. This feature would be especially useful in an environment where chemical clues are unlikely to endure for long due to the intense heat. The ultimate biological bonanza would be if it could be shown that the sand cat had enhanced auditory acuity at the frequency of the call of its main prey – the gerbil.

The dense hair on the soles of the sand cat's feet, which presumably aids movement on a sand substrate by cushioning the foot and preventing the cat from sinking into the sand, may also serve to dampen the sounds (if any) of the cat's movements. This would aid the sand cat in stalking prey like gerbils, which have very acute hearing due to their enlarged tympanic bullae. This hairy cushion also results in the sand cat's spoor showing no trace of the sole pads so typical of all other cats.

Pallid colouring is a well-known feature of desert mammals and birds of Africa and Arabia, as most have buff, sandy or greyish colours. Conversely, animals in high rainfall areas are richly coloured. The relationship between colour and humidity is known as Gloger's rule. In other cats, such as the leopard, cheetah and caracal, the animals of arid environs are much paler than those of higher rainfall areas. The incidence of melanism in leopards and servals is also greatest in high rainfall areas.

The function of the pallid desert colouring is not clearly understood. In many cases it can be related to camouflage, but this is not likely to be a major consideration in the case of nocturnal animals. Pallid colouring is also linked to physiological mechanisms for coping with high temperatures. Examples of other mechanisms evolved by mammals to survive in desert environments include a nocturnal lifestyle, living underground, and the means of coping with their bodies' internal water balance by deriving sufficient water from their food. Additional adaptations, such as concentrated urine and faeces to avoid moisture loss, are well studied in some mammals. To what extent any of these varied physiological or behavioural mechanisms are utilized by the sand cat is unknown, but it would make a fascinating field of study.

Gerbils are small rodents of the desert or arid zones, and form a mainstay of the diet of smaller predators like the sand cat.

The most secretive of all the continent's cats is the African golden cat which inhabits the rainforest of West and equatorial Africa. Although it has been known to science since 1827, the golden cat is as enigmatic now as it was then. Virtually nothing is known about its social life or behaviour in the wild, and very little is known about its choice of prey.

The African golden cat is a robust animal, with short, thick limbs, a relatively large head and a broad face with heavy jaws. Its hindquarters slope somewhat and it has a longer tail than other medium-sized cats such as serval, caracal and swamp cat. It carries its tail in much the same drooping style as the cheetah.

The colour and coat pattern of the golden cat is enormously variable. Its ground colour ranges from slate grey to a bright, golden brown or ochre-red, with smoky grey and yellowish variations in between. The degree to which its coat bears the spotted pattern, and the colour of the spots, are also highly variable. Some cats are densely covered in small dark spots or flecks; others have fewer, more scattered spots, which are larger and generally shapeless. The greyish cats usually have chocolate brown or black flecks or spots, and the reddish cats have brown or dark, liver-coloured spots. All of the colour forms of this cat have dark, linear blotches of colour on an otherwise whitish or off-white to cream-coloured belly and chest, with irregular broken bars or spots on the insides of the upper limbs. Melanistic or semi-melanistic individuals are known, but are rare.

These variations in colour follow an imprecise cline across the continent. At the western edge of its range in Senegal, and at the eastern edge of the range in East Africa, the cats are unspotted. In the main block of the Upper Guinean or West African rainforest from Sierra Leone to western Togo golden cats are invariably spotted. In Gabon and Cameroon there are both spotted and unspotted cats, and in the Congo basin the trend toward unspotted colour forms becomes dominant. Some authors have suggested that the western golden cats tend to be grey and the eastern forms reddish. Golden cats are, however, just as likely to be grey as red, regardless of where they occur. The colour is not a secondary sexual characteristic, as there is a roughly equal occurrence of grey and red cats among males and females alike.

To complicate the issue of colour variation in golden cats further, there are records of cats changing colour. One young female, which arrived at the London Zoo in 1906 from Freetown, Sierra Leone, was reported by

Opposite: Strong, thick limbs and a heavier jaw indicate that the African golden cat can probably take larger, stronger prey than the rodents and birds which form the bulk of its diet.
Above: The smoky grey, spotted coat colour is one of several varieties found in the African golden cat, and seems to be the more common form in Côte d'Ivoire.

Above: The African golden cat occupies the ecological niche of a fairly specialized predator in the rainforests of Africa. In Asia this niche is filled by the very similar Asiatic golden cat.
Opposite: In the rainforests of West Africa, as elsewhere, there are many other predatory species that compete with the smaller cats, be they lizards (above) or the much larger African python (below).

R I Pocock to have changed from reddish-brown to grey over a period of four months. Other writers have recorded the opposite, with grey cats being transformed to red as they grew older. The cause of the colour changes is not understood and is a most unusual phenomenon among mammals.

Many other mammals, such as male nyala antelope and male bushbuck, undergo striking colour changes as they mature. In those cases, however, the colour change is clearly linked to their maturation and their sex. Most cats are more strikingly patterned when young, such as lion cubs with their spots, but they lose the patterns as they age. Cheetah cubs are black when born, but acquire their spotted coat as part of the growth process. Carnivores of high latitudes, such as the Arctic fox and stoat, regularly moult to a white winter coat and dark summer coat, but this appears to involve a different physiological process to the colour changes recorded in golden cats. The jaguarundi, a South American cat, which is the least marked of all cats, also has two colour forms, a dark reddish form and a more usual greyish-buff form. As in the golden cat, this appears to be an expression of fairly stable polymorphism in the population. Among red foxes, also, there are the common red colours as well as various other shades through to a dark melanistic form.

In the case of the golden cat, however, colour changes are not linked to age, season, sex, climate or locality, and many golden cats do not undergo any colour change at all. Jonathan Kingdon suggests that as the colour changes seem to affect particular individuals only, they may be brought about by internal hormonal changes that have a socio-sexual significance. The exact mechanism of the colour change in African golden cats is unknown, however, and, like its significance, can only be guessed at.

This cat's colour pattern distribution has been interpreted as

evidence for recognizng two subspecies of African golden cat with a hybrid zone between them. In this scheme the spotted golden cats of the Upper Guinean forest zone are recognized as the subspecies *Profelis aurata celidogaster*, the generally unspotted cats east of the Congo River are regarded as subspecies *Profelis aurata aurata*.

The cats of the region between the upper Cross River at about 9 °E longitude and the Congo River, largely in Cameroon and Gabon, where both spotted and unspotted forms occur, are viewed as part of the 'hybrid' section between the two subspecies. Such an arrangement would imply a separation of one original parent population into two recognized forms. Although there is little evidence of this, we know that there have been extensions and contractions of the rainforest biome within the last million years, and even within the past 20 000 years there have been major changes related to pluvial periods where the forest expanded, and periods of aridity when the forest contracted and was discontinuous. The Dahomey Gap, which represents a complete break in the distribution of golden cats, was covered in forest during the height of the wetter periods which prevailed from

10 000 to 6 000 years ago. At such a time the African golden cat could have had a continuous distribution within a forest environment which has only relatively recently been broken by the emergence of the Gap, due to the upwelling of the cold Benguela current off the coast, which affects rainfall.

There is evidence that as recently as 18 000 years ago the African rainforest was reduced to five major refuges, with arid country between, with much of the Congo basin being covered by the Kalahari Desert. The largest of these refuges, as mapped by A C Hamilton, was in the Cameroon/Gabon area where the greatest diversity of golden cat coat patterns is found today, implying that the greatest degree of genetic diversity is present in this area. As one moves away from the centre of genetic diversity, the species shows less variation due to reduced genetic potential. Such an explanation has been advanced by Jonathan Kingdon as a plausible alternative to the scenario of the two subspecies for explaining the coat pattern variations shown by this enigmatic cat.

The golden cat is a forest inhabitant, and there are only a few records of its occurrence along the fringes of the rainforest. There are two isolated records of its being present well to the north of the forest block, one from Mali and one from Lake Chad, but these are from areas of atypical habitat, and could be based on trade skins which originated elsewhere.

Golden cats are thought to be more abundant in forest areas with dense undergrowth, such as those commonly found in secondary forest where the canopy has been cut down and regrowth is occurring. In these situations there is far more food available for their main prey species – such as rodents and duikers – than in primary forest where undergrowth is sparse. Golden cats are also found in riverine or gallery forest along the edge of the main forest zone. In these situations the rainforest biome extends along the well-watered banks of major rivers well into drier habitats. The mostly tropical climate of the golden cat's habitat is characterized by being hot and humid, with rainfall usually well above 1 000 millimetres a year and with rain falling during at least nine months of the year. In the Ruwenzori Mountains, on the border between Zaïre and Rwanda, golden cats occur in a much colder climate at altitudes of up to 2 000 metres above sea level. In the alpine vegetation of these mountains, the giant *Senecio adnivalis* and *Lobelia wollastoni* are the only large, woody plants. At lower altitudes in the East African mountains these cats are found in the dense bamboo forest zone, and even lower down in montane forest.

Very little is known about the ecology and behaviour of the African golden cat. Few Westerners have been fortunate enough to see live cats in the wild. Although the African forest peoples may have some knowledge of this cat's behaviour – passed on in oral tradition from generation to generation – hardly anything has appeared in print. Very few golden cats have ever been kept in captivity, and little has been recorded of the behaviour of those in zoos.

It is fair to assume, however, from the cat's anatomy, a few chance observations, and some of its recorded behaviour, that it can hunt competently in trees. It sometimes takes its prey, such as roosting birds, on the lower branches of forest trees, but it is equally adept at hunting on the ground. Kingdon records that in the Ruwenzoris golden cats prey mainly on rats, tree hyraxes and black-fronted duikers. Their terrestrial hunting habits are attested to by their frequently attacking duikers caught in snares. Golden cats also take monkeys and birds, such as guinea-fowl and francolin, which are presumably either stalked on the ground during the day or taken in the trees while the birds are roosting at night. In the Uturi forest of Zaïre, African golden cats have been recorded as feeding on blue duiker, pygmy antelope, bay duiker, giant forest squirrel, giant rat, chequered elephant shrew and birds of various kinds. In Uganda a golden cat was observed chasing a Peters' duiker. According to Jonathan Kingdon the golden cat raids poultry and also kills goats and sheep in recently settled areas of secondary forest in Uganda.

There appears to be considerable overlap in prey taken by African golden cats and leopards, where they occur in the same habitat. Despite this overlap and potential competition, the golden cat probably takes smaller prey than the leopard. There is evidence, cited by Jonathan Kingdon, that the golden cat prefers the dense undergrowth of secondary and disturbed forest, whereas the leopard is more likely to be found in primary forest.

Golden cats are secretive and largely nocturnal, although some have been seen out and about during the daylight hours. Normally they are solitary creatures, but Jonathan Kingdon has seen two adults together. In this respect they are much like other cats. Nothing is known about their social behaviour, other than an observation of two animals sunbathing together and grooming each other. Their territorial behaviour is unknown, but it is most likely to be somewhat like that of the leopard, albeit on a smaller scale.

The African golden cat is an alert animal with good hearing, eyesight and sense of smell – all of which allow it to avoid human observers. Captives hiss and snarl in anger, and growl and miaow like domestic cats.

Golden cat dung has been found on paths with no sign of scraping or attempts to cover it. This is probably indicative of its arboreal lifestyle, because if it normally defecates from a branch, it would be unable to cover its droppings as the serval does, for example.

There is only one record of an African golden cat kitten ever being found in the wild – with its mother in a den in a hollow fallen log. None have been trapped or killed by animal collectors. This is an indication that golden cats probably have their kittens in holes in trees, rather than in some ground shelter. There are also no known juvenile skins in any museum collections, probably indicating that the young stay well hidden and do not venture onto the ground where they can be trapped until they are well grown.

Paul and I were lucky enough to see a captive African golden cat in Abidjan when we visited the Côte d'Ivoire in search of elephant. The cat we saw was grey, heavily spotted, and it gazed at us calmly – its large green eyes only half open as it napped. In typical cat fashion it then yawned, opening its mouth wide to show us its formidable canines. At the time we did not realize just how rare this creature was – for there are no museum specimens from the Côte d'Ivoire, even though the species is well known in that country. Most of the skins and skulls in collections have been purchased from African hunters or rural markets. Museum collectors and professional animal trappers seldom come upon this highly elusive cat.

Opposite: In the complex ecology of the African rainforest, significant competition exists between leopards and African golden cats.
Above: White-collared mangabey monkeys of the rainforests may fall prey to African golden cats.

Nothing has as yet been published on precisely how the golden cat deals with its prey in the wild. Golden cats held in captivity have been observed grabbing birds with their claws and killing them with a bite to the back of the neck. They also pluck the feathers before eating. One assumes that, like most cats, the golden cat will make a careful stalk of its prey with a rapid rush and pounce on its victim. The only close relative of the African golden cat, the Asiatic golden cat, is reported to be most agile, with an excellent leaping ability. Apparently it also literally runs up and down vertical trees. The Asiatic golden cat is reported by E P Gee to prey on small mammals, birds, goats, sheep and even to take water buffalo calves on occasion.

Summary of biological data

This section presents a brief summary of the salient features with regard to the habitat, size, diet, reproduction and behaviour of Africa's cats. Brief reference is also made to the conservation status of each species. It is apparent from this summary that our knowledge of some of the smaller cats in particular is still scanty, while much more is known about the larger species. At the time of writing, the most comprehensive and up-to-date review of the literature relevant to African cats is the IUCN publication: *Wild Cats: Status Survey and Conservation Action Plan*, compiled and edited by Kristin Nowell and Peter Jackson in 1996.

We have attempted a rough indication of the distribution of individual cat species on the maps provided. It should be borne in mind, however, that the shaded areas can only be approximations of where the various species may be found. In addition, it must be noted that distribution does not necessarily occur evenly throughout the shaded areas, but rather that the cats are to be found in smaller pockets within the areas shown.

CHEETAH
ACINONYX JUBATUS

HABITAT Open grassland, semi-desert scrub, tree savanna and open woodlands.

SIZE Males 35–65 kg, 70–94 cm tall, 190–220 cm nose to tail tip. Females 36–63 kg, 185–220 cm nose to tail tip.

DIET Mostly small and medium-sized antelope and gazelle, the young of larger species and sometimes adults; hares, birds. Does not scavenge.

REPRODUCTION Gestation 90–95 days, 1–6 cubs, usually three. Weaned at 3–6 months, independent after 18 months.

BEHAVIOUR Females solitary and territorial; some males form territorial groups, others are solitary. Active during the day, usually hunts in early morning and late afternoon. Chases prey at speeds of up to 100 km per hour for short distances.

STATUS Suffers competition and depredation from other large carnivores; can exist on cattle farms and game ranches with enlightened management. Restricted genetic viability may increase vulnerability to disease epidemics. Red Data Book: out of danger in southern Africa, vulnerable worldwide. Appendix I of CITES.

SERVAL
LEPTAILURUS SERVAL

HABITAT Well-watered savanna and woodland areas with dense, tall grass and reed vegetation.

SIZE Males 10–18 kg, 54–62 cm tall, 96–120 cm from nose to tail tip. Females 9–13 kg, 95–120 cm nose to tail, and slightly smaller.

DIET Mostly larger rodents; occasionally small antelope, birds, reptiles, frogs.

REPRODUCTION Gestation 65–75 days, 1–3 kittens per litter. Independent at 6–8 months.

BEHAVIOUR Solitary, possibly territorial, active morning and evening (crepuscular).

STATUS Main threat is habitat destruction and, in particular, the disappearance of wetlands. Red Data Book: rare. Listed in Appendix II of CITES.

BLACK-FOOTED CAT
FELIS NIGRIPES

HABITAT Dry, short and medium-length grassland or open Karoid plains with some bushes or holes for cover.

SIZE The smallest African cat: males 1.5–2.4 kg, 16–25 cm tall, 54–69 cm nose to tail tip. Females 1–1.6 kg, 50–53 cm nose to tail tip.

DIET Mostly rodents and small birds; also mammals up to the size of hares and birds up to the size of korhaans; reptiles, invertebrates and occasionally birds' eggs.

REPRODUCTION Gestation 63–68 days, 1–3 kittens, sometimes two litters per year. Weaned at 6–8 weeks.

BEHAVIOUR Solitary, probably territorial, nocturnal.

STATUS Reasonably safe due to low commercial potential of its habitat. Red Data Book: rare. Appendix II of CITES.

AFRICAN WILD CAT
FELIS SILVESTRIS LYBICA

HABITAT Occurs in a wide range of habitats as long as some cover is available, thinly distributed in true desert and absent from dense forest.

SIZE Slightly larger than a house cat; males 4–5 kg, 35 cm tall, 85–100 cm long nose to tail tip. Females 3.2–5.5 kg, 82–95 cm long.

DIET Mostly rodents and other mammals up to the size of hares and the young of small antelope; birds, reptiles, amphibians and invertebrates.

REPRODUCTION Gestation 56–60 days, 2–5 kittens per litter at yearly intervals. Weaned at 2–3 months, independent by 5 months.

BEHAVIOUR Solitary, territorial, mostly nocturnal, although also active in the late afternoon and early morning.

STATUS Principal threat is hybridization with domestic cats. Red Data Book: vulnerable. Appendix II of CITES.

LEOPARD

PANTHERA PARDUS

HABITAT Occurs in all habitat types except true desert.

SIZE Males exceptionally up to 90 kg, typically about 60 kg, 70–80 cm tall, 160–190 cm nose to tail tip. Females up to 58 kg, typically about 32 kg, 64 cm tall, 190 cm nose to tail tip.

DIET Mammals from rodents to eland, with local specialities determined by available prey species abundance, favoured prey is in the 20–70 kg range; other vertebrates and insects.

REPRODUCTION Gestation 90–112 days, litters of 1–4 cubs, usually two or three. Weaned from 3 months, independent at 12 months or later.

BEHAVIOUR Solitary and territorial. Nocturnal.

STATUS A resilient species, safe in protected areas and able to exist alongside extensive agriculture. Displaced by intensive farming and settlement. Red Data Book: rare. Listed in Appendix I of CITES.

LION

PANTHERA LEO

HABITAT Most at home in open tree savanna or scrub savanna and woodland, not in true desert or dense forest.

SIZE Males up to 260 kg, usually about 190 kg, up to 120 cm tall and 2.5–3.3 m nose to tail tip. Females usually about 120 kg, 110 cm tall and 2.3–2.7 m nose to tail tip.

DIET Mostly large mammals 50–300 kg, up to buffalo, hippo and young elephants; also small mammals, birds, reptiles, fish; rarely people. Often scavenges, even driving predators such as leopard or cheetah off their kills and claiming them.

REPRODUCTION Gestation 98–110 days, 1–6 cubs, usually 1–4, at two-year intervals. Weaned at 7–8 months. Usually independent at about two years.

BEHAVIOUR Lives in prides consisting of 4–12 females and their young, with 1–6 males. Hunts in groups. Mostly active at night, rests up during the day in shade. Most males leave their natal pride at independence, while most females are incorporated into it as adults.

STATUS Common in large protected areas. Cannot co-exist with humans and livestock. Appendix II of CITES.

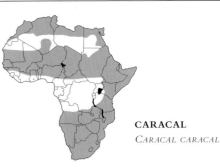

CARACAL

CARACAL CARACAL

HABITAT Avoids only true desert and dense forest, but most abundant in scrubby, arid habitats with broken or mountainous topography.

SIZE Males up to 20 kg, usually 11–17 kg, 40–45 cm tall, 100–130 cm nose to tail tip. Females 9–15 kg, 40 cm tall at the shoulder, 100–120 cm nose to tail tip.

DIET Mammals, including antelope up to 40 kg; birds, reptiles, invertebrates.

REPRODUCTION Gestation 64–68 days, 2–5 kittens per litter. Weaned at 4–6 months. Independent at about 12 months.

BEHAVIOUR Solitary, probably territorial, predominantly nocturnal.

STATUS Very resilient, even under pressure from vermin control. Displaced by intensive farming and settlement. Appendix II of CITES.

SWAMP CAT

FELIS CHAUS

HABITAT Reed beds and other lush vegetation in wet areas of the Nile Valley.

SIZE 5–13 kg, 40–48 cm tall at the shoulder, 85–130 cm nose to tail tip.

DIET Rodents, frogs, reptiles, birds and the young of larger mammals.

REPRODUCTION Gestation 56–66 days, 2–5 kittens per litter. Weaned at 8 weeks, independent after 5 months.

BEHAVIOUR Solitary, active during the day.

STATUS African population is at the edge of the species' range and is vulnerable to habitat destruction. More abundant in Asia. Appendix II of CITES.

SAND CAT

FELIS MARGARITA

HABITAT Sandy and stony desert with sparse vegetation.

SIZE Adults are 70–90 cm nose to tail tip, 25–30 cm tall. Males weigh 2.0–3.4 kg and females 1.5–3.0 kg.

DIET Rodents, in particular gerbils; small birds, reptiles, invertebrates and arthropods.

REPRODUCTION Gestation 50–63 days, 1–4 kittens per litter once a year. Independent at 10–12 months.

BEHAVIOUR Solitary, nocturnal, spending most of its time underground in burrows.

STATUS Probably safe because its habitat is only very sparsely populated by humans. Appendix II of CITES.

AFRICAN GOLDEN CAT

PROFELIS AURATA

HABITAT Primary and secondary forest and dense scrub up to high altitudes.

SIZE 11–18 kg, 50 cm tall, about 95–150 cm long nose to tail tip.

DIET Rodents and other mammals up to the size of duikers; birds.

REPRODUCTION Gestation 75 days, probably only one kitten per litter. Weaned from 6 weeks.

BEHAVIOUR Probably solitary and primarily nocturnal.

STATUS Safe as long as its forest habitat remains. Listed in Appendix II of CITES.

GLOSSARY

abiotic – devoid of life, a term applied to the non-living elements of the environment, e.g. rocks, soil and climate

arboreal – the lifestyle of animals that live in trees or are adapted to life in trees

articulated bones – the limb bones

biomass – the total mass of organisms living in a given area, expressed as mass per unit area, e.g. kg/ha

biome – one of a number of broad ecological units on earth distinguished by a particular mix of landforms, climate, plant and animal species, e.g. desert or forest

biotic – relating to life, a term applied to all living organisms, e.g. bacteria, animals and plants

bush – in Africa this commonly refers to a wilderness area of natural vegetation with wildlife, as opposed to settled areas

canopy – the upper zone or 'roof' of a forest, formed by the branches of neighbouring trees overlapping and touching

conspecifics – organisms belonging to the same species

crepuscular – active at twilight, as opposed to being diurnal or nocturnal

cursorial – of the chase, designed for running

'dear-enemy' – the animal behaviour of individual recognition of territorial neighbours resulting in keeping aggressive interactions or territorial battles to a minimum. Intensive aggression is reserved for strangers. Also described as the 'rival-friend' phenomenon.

density – the size of a population relative to a definite unit of space

diurnal – active during the daytime

ecology – the scientific study of the interactions of animals or plants with their environment, both biotic and abiotic

ecosystem – all of the interacting organisms and elements, both biotic and abiotic, of a particular type of habitat, e.g. forest or savanna

feral – formally domestic or captive animals which establish themselves in the wild

flehmen – a facial expression with lip pulled back and nose wrinkled adopted by the males of some animals when sniffing the urine or scent of oestrous females, or when smelling other socially important scent marks, e.g. territorial marks

gallery forest – the band of forest lining the banks of rivers, usually in the tropics

genotype – the genetic constitution of an individual organism

habitat – the locality or external environment in which an organism lives

home range – the area that an animal occupies and patrols regularly, but does not necessarily defend against conspecifics. The part of the home range that is defended constitutes the territory.

Karoo – the vast inland plains of South Africa, characterized by low rainfall and vegetation dominated by dwarf shrubs and grasses

kin selection – genetic selection brought about by individuals favouring or disfavouring the survival and reproduction of relatives (other than offspring) who, due to common descent, possess the same genes

macchia – a term used for the vegetation known in South Africa as 'fynbos', essentially shrub vegetation of winter rainfall areas

melanism/melanistic – darkness of colour in fur or feathers due to the pigment melanin

montane – occurring on mountains and areas above 1 500 m, usually in the eastern part of Africa

multimammate – term used to describe a species of mouse that has up to twelve pairs of nipples

nomadic animals – animals that move around irregularly in response to an environmental stimulus, e.g. rainfall, not necessarily returning to their original point of departure

orbits – the depressions in the skull in which the eyes are set

perineal – pertaining to the perineum, the space between the anus and genital organs

polyoestrous – completing two or more oestrus cycles in each sexual season

population – animals or plants of the same species occupying a clearly delimited area at a particular time

pug marks – old-fashioned term used to describe the spoor of large cats like lions and tigers. It originated in India.

rainforest – in Africa it is the evergreen, tropical lowland forest where the annual rainfall is at least 1 200 mm and with no more than two months receiving less than 50 mm of rain

relict – in the sense of a population, one that is isolated in space or time

rival-friend – the same form of behaviour as described under 'dear-enemy'

Sahel – a broad band of arid vegetation which stretches across Africa from east to west and which separates the Sahara desert from the better-watered savanna and woodland to the south

species – the basic unit of taxonomic classification consisting of individuals or populations that are capable of freely interbreeding with one another (but not with other species under natural conditions) and producing fertile young

sympatric – species or populations with at least partially overlapping geographical ranges

territory – an area occupied exclusively by an animal or group of animals and from which conspecifics are excluded by defence or display

thicket – a very dense, almost impenetrable community of trees and/or large shrubs

veld – word of South African origin meaning fairly open country, not under cultivation or forested; also used in the same sense as the American 'range'

ACRONYMS USED IN THE TEXT

CITES – Convention on International Trade in Endangered Species of Fauna and Flora (Washington Convention)

IUCN – International Union for the Conservation of Nature and Natural Resources

IUCN/SSC – Species Survival Commission of the IUCN

WWF – World Wide Fund for Nature

CAT CONTACTS

There are several organizations devoted to the conservation or rehabilitation of cats, or to research on them or to the conservation of their habitat. All would welcome donations to the funding of their work. Contact can be made with them at the following addresses:

IUCN/SSC
  Cat Specialist Group
Chairman: Peter Jackson
IUCN
World Conservation Centre
Avenue Mont Blanc
1196 Gland, Switzerland

De Wildt Cheetah Research
  Centre
P O Box 16
De Wildt 0251
South Africa

Wildcare (incorporating
  Animal Rehabilitation Centre)
P O Box 15121
Lynne East 0039
South Africa

African Carnivore Survey
P O Box 6
Loxton 6985
South Africa

WWF South Africa
P O Box 456
Stellenbosch 7599

Chipangali Wildlife Trust
P O Box 1057
Bulawayo
Zimbabwe

The Africat Foundation
P O Box 793
Otjiwarongo
Namibia

Cheetah Conservation Fund
P O Box 247
Windhoek
Namibia

Cheetah Conservation Fund
2162 Baldwin Road
Ojai
California 93123
USA

SELECTED BIBLIOGRAPHY

Our knowledge of African cats has been built up over the years in the bush and in close contact not only with wildlife but with people who live close to wildlife. However, in writing a book such as this it is necessary to use the published work of others as a source of information, interpretation and ideas. We gratefully acknowledge the work of others and here provide some of the more important texts which have guided us, and can be depended upon by any reader wishing to explore the world of African cats in greater depth. In this regard the foremost, essential works are those of Kingdon, Rosevear and Ewer – each of whom has made an enormous contribution to our knowledge of African mammals. Jonathan Kingdon's work in particular is always thought-provoking and inspirational. Furthermore, there are hundreds of reports and papers in scientific journals dealing with Africa's cats. We list here a few field guides, species studies and general background works on Africa.

BAILEY, T. N. 1993. *The African Leopard: Ecology and Behaviour of a Solitary Felid.* Columbia University Press: New York.

BROWN, L. 1965. *Africa. A Natural History.* Hamish Hamilton: London.

CARO, T. M. 1994. *Cheetahs of the Serengeti Plains: Group Living in an Asocial Species.* University of Chicago Press: Chicago and London.

DORST, J. and DANDELOT, P. A. 1970. *Field Guide to the Larger Mammals of Africa.* Collins: London.

DUPUY, A.R. 1971. *Le Niokolo-Koba, Premier Grand Parc National de la République du Sénégal.* G.I.A.: Dakar.

EWER, R.F. 1973. *The Carnivores.* Weidenfeld and Nicolson: London.

GROBLER, H., HALL-MARTIN, A. and WALKER, C. 1989. *Predators of Southern Africa. A Field Guide.* Second Edition. Southern Book Publishers: Johannesburg.

HALTENORTH, T. and DILLER, H.A. 1984. *Field Guide to the Mammals of Africa including Madagascar.* Collins: London.

HAMILTON, P.H. 1981. The Leopard *Panthera pardus* and the Cheetah *Acinonyx jubatus* in Kenya. *Report for the U.S. Fish and Wildlife Service.* African Wildlife Foundation and Government of Kenya.

HARRISON, D.L. 1977. *The Mammals of Arabia. Vol. II. (Carnivora. Artiodactyla. Hyracoidea).* Ernest Benn: London.

HART, J.A. KATEMBO, A. and PUNGA, K. 1996. Diet, prey selection and ecological relations of leopard and golden cat in the Ituri forest, Zaïre. *African Journal of Ecology* 34 (4): 364–379.

KINGDON, J. 1977. East African Mammals. *An Atlas of Evolution in Africa. Vol. III. Part A (Carnivores).* Academic Press: London and New York.

KINGDON, J. 1990. *Arabian Mammals. A Natural History.* Academic Press: London.

KINGDON, J. 1997. *The Kingdon Field Guide to African Mammals.* Academic Press: San Diego and London.

MOREAU, R.E. 1996. *The Bird Faunas of Africa and its Islands.* Academic Press: New York and London.

NEFF, N.A. 1982. *The Big Cats. The Paintings of Guy Coheleach.* Harry N. Abrams: New York.

NOWELL, K. and JACKSON, P. 1996. *Wild Cats. Status Survey and Conservation Action Plan.* IUCN/SSC Cat Specialist Group, IUCN: Gland, Switzerland.

ROSEVEAR, D.R. 1974. *The Carnivores of West Africa.* British Museum (Natural History): London.

SCHALLER, G.B. 1972. *The Serengeti Lion. A Study of Predator–Prey Relations.* University of Chicago Press: Chicago and London.

SCOTT, J. 1985. *The Leopard's Tale.* Elm Tree Books: London.

SHORTRIDGE, G.C. 1931. *The Mammals of South West Africa. Vol. I.* William Heineman: London.

SMITHERS, R.H.N. 1983. *The Mammals of the Southern African Subregion.* University of Pretoria: Pretoria.

STUART, C.T. and WILSON, V.J. 1988. *The Cats of Southern Africa.* Chipangali Wildlife Trust: Bulawayo.

VAN DYK, A. 1991. *The Cheetahs of De Wildt.* Struik Publishers: Cape Town.

WHITE, F. 1983. *The Vegetation of Africa. A Descriptive Memoire to Accompany the Unesco/AETFAT/UNSO Vegetation Map of Africa.* Unesco: Paris.

WOZENCROFT, W.C. Order Carnivora, in Wilson, D.E. and Reeder, D.M. (Eds.). 1993. *Mammal Species of the World: A Taxonomic and Geographic Reference.* Second Edition. Smithsonian Institution Press: Washington D.C. and London.

LIST OF SUBSCRIBERS

SPONSORS' EDITION

Babich Family
Steve Bales
E. Bertelsmann SC
Angela Blanden
Adrian H. Bosman
Paul & Elaine Bosman
In memory of,
Peter Hathaway Capstick
Peter Flack

Steve Hall
Gideon Holtzhausen
John Jacobs
Friedrich Krachler
Allan & Anna Kronenburg
Peter Martens
Michael & Norma Rattray
Robin Moser
Jan & Elizabeth Nel
Marc Péchenart

RASCO Investment Trust
River Ranges
Michael F. Sharman
Mr & Mrs Michael Steele
& Family
Total South Africa
Jean Turck
Leo. van den Heever
Mrs Jean Waggoner

COLLECTORS' EDITION

G. Angelini
W.A. Bailey
William Barlow
Rodrick Barongi
Diana L. Barrell
Viv & Lori Bartlett
Bill Boyd & Pat Bayley
C.H. Berman
R.J.S. Borlase
Joan S. Bortnick
Christopher Bosman
Kate Bosman
Simon Bosman
Kevin, Odette & Tarryn
    Bourhill
Sheldon V. Brooks
Ian Bishop & Kerry-Anne
    Chambers
C.J. Chorlton
Cowabunga Clarke
Hugh & Connie Coble
John & Brenda Collett

Donald & Rosemary Currie
Famille E. Dandrieux
W.H.J. de Beer
Paul H. Deniger
Grant & Caroline Donaldson
Dr Anthony Hall-Martin
Johan & Sarah du Plessis
J.P. du Plessis
Endangered Wildlife Trust
Fernwood Press (Pty)
    Limited
First National Bank
Dr Alby J. Ford
Mr & Mrs M.C. Fox
John & Candy Fraser
E.S.C. Garner
Lydia Gorvy
Patricia & Alan Graham-Collier
Alec & Cathy Grant
Elizabeth B. Henry
John K. Hepburn
Richard Hill

Rupert, Nadia, Brett, Grant
    & Dylan Horley
C.R. Hunting
L.R. Hunting
M.S. Hunting
Neville Renè Jenkinson
Chris & Jeanne Jennings
G.E. Jewell
Ben Jonker
M.F. Keeley
Dr Harold König,
    Pretoria Eye Institute
Nora Kreher
Albert E. Kuschke
Mike G. Lourens
Morris Lurie
Robert Maingard
Thomas Walter Martin
Edward J. Maruska
John McCormick
Linda & Tony Meakin
Allen & Carol Miller

George Moggach
Robin Moser
Karl-Heinz Müller
Tim & Jenny Newsome
L-M. Nicholls
Peter & Audrey Nyman
Danie, Anet, Daniel, Christiaan,
    Loren & Rita Olivier
Michael A. Oughtibridge
Ian Outram
Petersfield Nurseries
Dr & Mrs D.G.C. Presbury
Dr W.L. Pretorius, Kimberley,
    South Africa
Tanya M. Price
Dudley Proctor, African
    Wildlife Library
H. Prokas
Dirk Raath
Dr Ludger Reißig
J.L. Rochér
Con en Jacqueline Schabort

Lawrence Schoen
Kenneth Scriven
David & Cailey Selwyn,
    Australia
Hanno Sierts
Dr Alf Smith Jr
Kathleen Lamont Smith
James M. Southey
Robert M. Thomas Jr
Mr Kunj Trivedi
Geoffrey Ulrich
Glenn van Heerden
J.A. Janse van Rensburg
N.P. Janse van Rensburg
W. van Rÿswÿck
M. & A. van Sandwyk
Dr C.L. Venter
Peter & Jeffe Williams
Trisha Wilson
J.A. Windell
Aubrey & Elizabeth
    Wynne-Jones

STANDARD EDITION

A B C Bookshop
L.J. Admiraal
Ivonne & Oswald Albers
M. Alberts
Nardus Alberts
Mrs S. Alberts
Keith Allen
Antonio Federico Alziati
Amcoal Colliery & Industrial
    Operations Limited
Michael & Monica Amm
Mark Amos
Dr Ellen Ancker
Mr & Mrs D.J. Anderson
Dr Ingram F. Anderson

Peter Apps
Brian Askew
H. Elvey Austen
Norval Ray Babcock
Ivan Babaya
Derek & Karen Badenhorst
F.G. Bakker
David & Linda Baldie
Marijke & Ken Ball
Jörg Bandholtz
K.R. Baragwanath
Ken & Maggie Barker
Lisa Hywood Barnard
Bert Barnes
Rodrick Barongi

J.H. Barrie
Brian W. Batchelor
Duncan Bates, Eagle's Rest Farm,
    Cape Point
Lance Batho
Pieter Bedford
Reinher-H. Behrens
Kathy Beling
Keith, Lesley, Trevor & Stuart Bell
Angiolo Bellini
I. Bergh
Peter & Marliese Berndt
Henry Bernitz
M.J. Bester
Professor Gerhard & Isolde Beukes

Christine Beyers
Danie & Ina Bezuidenhout
Clive Biden
M.A. Billing
Mike & Cynthia Black
Cheryl Pratten & Simon Blackburn
Hilton Blake
Grant L. Blanden
Diederict M. Blankenmeijer,
    The Netherlands
K. Blatherwick
Keith & Wendy Bloy
Julie Boddy
Mrs N. Bolton
E.L. Booysen

Chris & Norma Boshoff
André J. Botha
J. du P. Bothma
C.J. Bouwer
Paul & Rachael Bower
William Miles Dugard Bowker
Dr J. Bradley
P.F. Brink
Hylton Briscoe
Andrew Brock-Doyle
Anthony & Frances Broekhuizen
Gordon & Ann Brooker
Ian & Kaye Brown
P.M. Brown
J.A. Bruckner

John D. Bryce
David Buchan
Laetitia Buchner
Beverley Bunch
Chris Burchmore
John & Penny Burchmore
Alwyn & Joyce Burger
Boet & Yvonne Burger
Henri, Engela, Jacques & Nandi Burger
Dr Carolyn Burhenn
Fay & Roy Burrett
Peter Burroughes
Grant Burton
Carl Buss
Derek & Carol Butcher
Alan & Joanne Calenborne
Mrs Rita Calvert
Neil & Val Card
Mr Luca Causa
Deborah Chambers
P.J. Cillié
G.B. Clapham
Betty C. Clark
Ms C.M. Claude
Volkert Clausen
Elizabeth A. Clayton
P.A.G. Cloete
Dr P.G. Close
A.P.C. Coetsee
E.T. Coetzee
Johann & Steph Coetzee
M.J.R. Coetzee
Dean Russell Coetzer
C.B. Colbourne
Des & Naureen Cole
Sue Collins
The Columbine Family
J.M. Copeman
Dr Graham Coupland
Brian Courtenay
Guy & Yvonne Courtin
Graham & Jillian Cox
Robert Crausaz
Matthew Crean
Ian Crocker
Annabel Crook
Paul Crosland
R.D. Cruse
Richard & Stephanie Cunliffe
Mr & Mrs A.P. Currie
Harold H. Currie
A.D. Damelin
Andre Darmont, Waremme, Belgium
Robbin Davies
R.E. & G. Dawson
Richard & Maureen de Beer
Dr John N. de Beer
Nico J. de Beer
M.D.B. de Greeff
André de Haan
Bennet en Chantalle de Klerk
André & Yvonne de Kock

D.D. de Kock
C.J. de Lange
Kees & Loes de Lind Wijngaarden,
    The Netherlands
D. de Milander
J.C. (Kay) de Villiers
Peter & Dyanne de Vos
Mr J.F. de Wet Jr (Cobie)
Maureen & Dudley Deeks
Michael, Ingrid, Gabriella & Rafaela
    Dennill
Gill Dewar
Helen Dewar
Sara Dewar
Jalal & Kulsum Dhansay
Martin, Lisa & Vincent Di Bella
Hendrik & Coba Diederiks
Karen V. Dixon
W.R. Doepel
Karen Dörnbrack
Graeme Dott
Tony & Wendy Drake
Dr J.C. Dreyer, Rondom, Vredendal
Charl du Plessis
Mr & Mrs René du Plessis
Francois du Randt
Flick du Toit
R.F. du Toit
Trevor N. Duckham
Dr N. Dunstone
Jon Eagar
A.K. Edgecombe
Robert T. Edwards
Fritz Eisoldt
Gert A. Eksteen
Vasili Eleftheriou
Mr & Mrs R.G. Elliott-Darlow
Professor Fritz Eloff
Dr John Eloff
Kenneth S. Else
Mr & Mrs Mark Embleton
Anton O. Endres
Amos Eno
Barend F.N. Erasmus
Carla & Felix Ernst
Mike & Liz Ettmayr
John L. Evens
C.P. Everitt
G.L. Faber
Bruce Vincent Falck
Pauline Farquhar
Ann Farrow
Gavin & Antoinette Faulds
G.T. Ferreira
Khakie Ferreira
Liz & Alex Fick
Carolyn Figueiredo
First National Bank
Glenn Fischer
Peter & Sue Fitt
J. & D. Flack
Gareth John Ford

Mrs D. Forman
Beverley Anne Fourie
Marchant Fourie
T.S. Fourie
W.P. Frost
Malcolm Funston
Paul Funston
John Furniss
Peter B. Gain
Kevin Gallagher
Antonio Garcia-Alonso,
    Almeria, Spain
Iain Garratt
Jerry Garrett
Rendall Garrett
Francois Geldenhuys
Michael Georgiou Family
F.A. Gerber
Alice Gilbert
Albert Earl Gilbert
Sarah Godsell
Martha Going
E. Goodyear
Mr & Mrs J.D. Goodyear
Mel Goott
Major I.A.D. Gordon M.B.E.
T.P. & G.R.N. Gordon-Cumming
James & Trish Gordon-Lennox
Jerry Gosnell, Mhlosinga Nature
    Reserve
Ken Graham
F.E. Graves
A. Gray
A.H. Green
Chris & Sonja Greyvensteyn
D.G. Griffin & Family
Jors & Mariet Grobler
The Grundy Family
The Gurnell Family
Mr & Mrs D.A. Hall
Izak Hanekom, Ceres
Rudolf, Sonia & Savannah Hanni
Wolf-George Harms, Germany
Paul Ian Harris
Louise & Robert Harrison
Marcelle Harrison
M.S. Harrold
J.O.C. Hart
R.A. Harvey
G.R. Havers
Renée Hawes
Michael Hearn
Carin Herbert
Bernard Heritage
Anne Heukelman
R. Hickman
C.O. Hill
Mr & Mrs E.H.O. Hoal
P.B. Hodes
N. Holden
Herman & Maria Holleman,
    Holland

Lex Trust Hollmann
Tineke Honig-Van der Meulen
Diana Hood
Raymond J.L. Hoog
Eric Howes
Torrence M. Hunt
Ian B. Huntley
Joan & Robin Hutchinson
Doug & Jane Hutson
John Huxter
Brig. D.J.D. Jacobs
F.A. Jacobs
John Jacobs
A. Jagga
Ron & Jenny James & Family
R.F. Jeffery
David F. Jenkins
G.W. Johnson
George J. Johnston, Carmichael,
    Ca., USA
M.G. Johnstone
Olga Jones
Shirley Jones
L.A. Joos-Vandewalle
David & Maé Jordaan
Inez Jordan
R.A. Kadur
Hillel M. Kahn
Sidney H. Kahn
Brian & Dil Kalshoven
Gabriel Kant, Berne, Switzerland
Ian Kavanagh
Derek Keats
Aliki & Clive Kelly
Paul Kennedy
Rodney Kenyon
Kimberley Boys' High School
B.J. Kirby
Linchen Kirchner
S.J.S. Klagsbrun
Yvette Klein
Roy & Erica Knickelbein
David & Noleen Knott
Leoné Koekemoer
Joan Krause
Philip J. Krawitz
C. Krog
Franci & Mariaan Krone
Bruce W. Krucke
Jan & Hazel Kruger
Günter Kruth
S. Kumaranayagam, Sri Lanka
William N. Lane III
John & Moira Lauderdale
Michael Lawrenson
R.M. Lawrie
Joy & Eric Le Huquet
Francois le Roux
Ina le Roux
Pierre & Sylvia le Roux
Jane & Patrick Ledin
Chris & Nicci Lenferna

John Lennard
Geoff & Billie Leslie
Professor L.J. Levien
S.S.E. Lewis
F.K.E. Lichtenberg
Rolf Liechti
Lionel Lindsay
Ian Hamilton Little
Lynton & Iris Lockwood-Hall
I.U. Lohmann
Betty Louw
David A. Louw
John W. Louw
Sandra Louw
Jamie & Yvonne Lovemore
Nicole Ludeke
Richard Ludeke
Mr J. E. Lumsden
Keith Lyon
Basie Maartens
Tracy-Lynne Ruth MacGregor
O.J. Mackenzie
Peter & Yvonne MacQuilkan
Cally Mail
Mala Mala Game Reserve
Johann H. Malan en Gesin
Francois Malherbe
Professor J.M. Malloch-Brown,
    Pretoria
Pauline & Leon Maltz
Colette Marais
Ivonne Marais
J. Marais
Dr S.J. Marais
Dr Jonathan Marchand
Dr Paul Marchand
Mrs C.S.M. Maree
Mr & Mrs J.H. Maree
P.J.H. Maree
Olga & Bill Marsay
Colin Marshall
Dr Charles A. Martin
D.G. Martin
Robbie & Lyn Massey-Hicks
Carlos Matos-Lopes
Victoria Matthews
A. Mavrandonis
Margaret & Bruce McBride
The McCarthy Family
B. McCormick
Candace E. McIntosh
Sean McKeag
Alexander McKerrow
Ryan McKerrow
M.G. McLean
Karen McLennan
Waynne & Tammy McLintock
S.E. McNeill
Mr I.B. McWalter
Linda & Tony Meakin
Nicóle Meiring
M.A. Meredith